# AUTISTICALLY AWESOME

## AUTISTICALLY AWESOME

Copyright © 2020 Ericka Wharton

ALL RIGHTS RESERVED. No part of this book may be reproduced, distributed, or transmitted in any form or by any means, including photocopying, recoding, or other electronic or mechanical methods, without the prior written permission from the author and certain other non-commercial uses permitted by copyright law.

Ordering Information

Special discounts are available on quantity purchases by corporations, schools,

libraries, and others. For details, contact the author.

Library of Congress Cataloging- in-Publication has been applied for.

ISBN-13: ISBN: 978-1-7346503-1-0

ISBN-10: 1734650310

PRINTED IN THE UNITED STATES OF AMERICA.

# TABLE OF CONTENTS

Chapter 1: **Acceptance** *"Easing Your Mind"* ............ 1

Chapter 2: **Signs, Symptoms, And Sensory:** *"What The Behaviors Look Like"* ............ 9

Chapter 3: **Parental Fears** *"You're Not Alone"* ............ 15

Chapter 4: **Needs And Wants** *"Differences Between Needs And Wants"* ............ 19

Chapter 5: **How The Brain Is Known To Work** *"Executive Functioning"* ............ 23

Chapter 6: **Important Steps To Take** *"Things To Do"* .... 31

Chapter 7: **Strategies And Interventions** *"Which Are Most Effective And Utilized?"* ............ 55

Chapter 8: **Helpful Programs/Services** *"Networking And Researching"* ............ 61

Chapter 9: **Common Goals To Work On** *"Most Effective And Appropriate Goals To Focus"* ............ 67

Chapter 10: **Different Levels** *"Depending On Behaviors And Sensory"* ............ 71

Chapter 11: **Crisis Identification** *"What Antecedents Took Place"* ............ 79

Chapter 12: **Behavior Plans/Charts** *Pecs* ............ 89

Chapter 13: **Scenarios/Case Studies 1** *"Nonverbal/Physical Aggressive Elementary Student"* ............ 93

My Collaborating Journey ............ 103

Conclusion ............ 109

Appendix: Important Terms/Definitions ............ 111

# Author Biography

Ericka Wharton is a Licensed Behavioral Specialist who is licensed with the Pennsylvania State Board of Medicine. Ericka is from Norristown, Pennsylvania, and comes from a strong family unit that shows love and support. Ericka has five beautiful children, of which the youngest was diagnosed with ASD and ADHD, and this makes Ericka his strongest advocate. It also attributes to her eleven years of experience as a Licensed Behavioral Specialist. Ericka is excited to assist and bridge the gaps between families and professionals for children who have been given the diagnosis of ASD.

# FOREWORD

I am honored to write this foreword, not only because Ericka Wharton has worked for me as a Licensed Behavioral Specialist for the past three years, but also because Ericka has been a successful contributor and professional in the Human Services Field for over 18 years. Ericka Wharton is qualified to write Autistically Awesome not only because of her professional experiences for the past 11 + years, but due to the fact that she has a child who is diagnosed with Autism, which she can share real life experiences both on a personal and professional level.

Autistically Awesome is an excellent read that is resourceful and extremely informative about Autism Spectrum Disorder. Ericka Wharton has done a tremendous job capturing important facts, based on her close engagements and interactions with many individuals who are diagnosed with Autism Spectrum Disorder. Ericka continues to support and expose important information for readers and the audience regarding topics that ranges from what happens when a child fails to meet developmental milestones to obtaining services for a child or youth to young adulthood who is diagnosed with this exceptionality.

Whether you are a caretaker or professional who is seeking information about an individual who is diagnosed with Autism Spectrum Disorder, this book will help you *"ease your mind"* by empowering you to remove the guilt you may have, so that you can continue caring for an exceptional individual with special needs, or if you are a professional in the Human Services Field; looking to become more informed about Autism, which this educational book "Autistically Awesome" covers the important steps you need to know when understanding or confirming that the individual is diagnosed with Autism Spectrum Disorder.

Autistically Awesome is an easy read because it gets straight to the point, uses language that the readers will be able to understand, the information is relevant due to the vast amount of children who are currently being diagnosed with Autism, and once you start reading you will not want to put it down. If you don't know much about Autism Spectrum Disorder, I highly recommend you to enjoy this book so that you can become more familiar with the diagnosis.

**Avia Tomlinson, M.Ed, LPC, Program Director**

# Chapter 1
# <u>Acceptance</u>
## *"Easing Your Mind"*

When a child's development and milestones do not fall within the expected range during the infancy and toddler stages, a variety of factors that include; lack of sensory, stimulation and preoccupation, as well as lack of age appropriate social skills can be identified as possible characteristics of these infants and toddlers. Depending on the concerns that exist, the parent or legal guardian also known as the caretaker of the child may need to consult a professionally licensed individual who specializes in pediatric and adolescent development for assistance. This individual will be able to recommend appropriate steps and evaluations to determine services available to aid the child. By partnering with someone experienced in this area, caretakers can avoid comparing their offspring to other children. A child with Autism Spectrum Disorder (ASD) should not be compared to other children; however, it is sometimes helpful to analyze the trends of different behaviors, keeping in mind that every typical and atypical individual should be individualized.

Parents are repeatedly told by those around them, "DO NOT BLAME YOURSELF!" Although it is common for caregivers to put blames on themselves, they should also connect with local services, support groups, and/or other parents. Networking, researching, and sharing data with others increases the caregiver's knowledge base and maximizes their opportunities to find something that will help their child. When people with similar plights gather, questions start to transpire. Questions arise because individuals want to validate what they feel is accurate. Some of the usual questions are: Is ASD genetic or environmental? Is it from immunizations? Where did it originate? The questions are endless, especially when the person affected is their child or another family member.

In society today, there are many arguments and disagreements regarding children who are diagnosed with any of the exceptionalities that exist, especially the exceptionality of ASD. Autism Spectrum Disorder has become very broad and in-depth. DSM V (Diagnostic and Statistical Manual of Mental Disorders) $5^{th}$ Edition (2013) discusses a variety of deficiencies and behaviors. Among the behaviors discussed is the lack of engagement, social skills, eye contact, and communication skills exhibited by individuals with ASD.

Arguments about the origination and establishment of ASD continue. Whether or not ASD evolved from the environment, genetics, or immunizations administered to infants and toddlers remains unknown because the research is incomplete. The arguments are ongoing and fueled by the personal opinions of individuals. Rather than focusing on its origination, the focus should be on appropriate strategies, treatment, and services that enable those diagnosed with ASD to function in their everyday lives.

It is beneficial professionally and personally to establish a relationship with children who are diagnosed with ASD. Multiple diagnoses that include a diagnosis of ASD can be very challenging for a parent or caregiver, but they should never give up! Help can be found with proper research and recommendations. Every second, minute, hour, day, week, month, and year brings new experiences that allow the parent or caregiver to add to their skillset and become experts in appropriate ASD strategies. As the children grow, their needs and daily routines will change, requiring adjustments by the caregiver.

Upon hearing the diagnosis of Autism, parents have many questions: What should I think? How should I feel? What should I expect? How will I help my child? What steps should I take? These are valid questions when thinking of the ASD diagnosis. Without prior knowledge or the understanding of ASD, people may experience some struggles, anxiety, challenges, and frustrations. Learning to understand and manage an individual(s) exhibiting specific behaviors that a child with ASD displays daily is a challenge.

Some caregivers may disagree with their child's diagnosis of Autism Spectrum Disorder. Despite a child's ability to academically exceed expectations, interact well with others, and follow instructions, he or she may still be a candidate for a diagnosis of ASD. This child would be categorized as high functioning. Children in this category may still face challenges with tantrums, meltdowns, or have issues with sensory (touch, taste, sight, sense, or smell).

If a child receives the ASD diagnosis, many factors have been documented by a licensed professional who felt the results indicated the child fell within the necessary levels to make an ASD diagnosis.

It can be difficult for a caregiver with no knowledge of Autism Spectrum Disorder to accept an ASD diagnosis. Accepting the ASD diagnosis means accepting that a child lacks in the development of social and coping skills. Children with ASD may be withdrawn to himself and have sensory deficiencies. They may have hyperactive and impulsive behaviors, as well as consistent, and repetitious movements.

Autism Spectrum Disorder is a lifelong diagnosis that isn't curable. It is important to understand how to guide and implement appropriate strategies and interventions that will work for each child. Depending on the way a child thinks and displays specific behaviors, caregivers can implement appropriate expectations with the use of visual aids.

Some steps can be taken during and after the diagnosis process. After receiving concerns from a licensed professional, family, or friends or recommendations for alternative educational placement, or even if they have speculation, a parent or caregiver should consider doing the following:

- If the child is 0–3 years of age, reach out to Early Interventions.
- If the child is 3–5 years old, reach out to your local Intermediate Unit.
- After completion of a full questionnaire for parents, daycare, or an educational environment, an intake will be completed.
- The questionnaire will be reviewed by a licensed professional and an appointment will be scheduled.
- At the appointment, the child will be observed by an occupational therapist, speech therapist, physical therapist, as well as a psychologist.

- Some of these individuals will visit the child's home to observe and review the questionnaire prior to their appointment at the local Intermediate Unit/location.

- The parent or caregiver will receive an I.F.S.P./I.E.P. (Individualized Family Service Plan) or (Individualized Education Plan) with diagnosis. After receiving the diagnosis, the child can begin receiving the eligible services and additional appointments can be set up.

- The caregiver should locate a Developmental Pediatrician so they can follow the child's development.

- If the child has a behavioral concern or challenges, local agencies can assist with wraparound services. They will schedule an Extended Assessment and provide the child with services using their observations and the information given by the caregiver.

- If the child struggles with speech, occupational and physical therapies, the caregiver can GOOGLE local establishments for outpatient therapies, such as TheraPlay.

- It will be helpful to network with other parents in local support groups, social media, or local libraries.

- Psychiatric assistance is also available. If the child needs medication(s) administered, an appointment should be made to discuss with educational staff. Medication(s) may be required for the child if they have moderate to severe levels of being hyperactive,

noncompliant, moody, or any other concerning behaviors.
- To ensure continuous care, the caretaker should make appropriate appointments.

Making appointments with the many professionals mentioned above may be repetitive, but it is necessary to ensure that everyone remains on the same page. Most professionals are still researching ASD and will ask about the family history of the individual. The parent or caregiver may be asked some of the following questions regarding the individual's history:

- Head injuries?
- Surgeries?
- Seizures?
- Serious injuries?
- Continuous headaches?
- Heart, hearing, or vision issues?
- Allergies?
- Feeding, digestive, or nutritional problems?
- G.I. problems?
- Dental or breathing problems?
- Neurological problems?
- Sickle Cell or any additional medical problems?

The process can be long and draining, but information gathered will be valuable to the experts. Autism Spectrum Disease is very broad, and its complexity continues to grow. Learning what to expect after the ASD diagnosis and accepting feedback from others will increase the caregiver's knowledge and skillset.

# Chapter 2
# **Signs, Symptoms, and Sensory:**
## *"What the Behaviors Look Like"*

The scope of an ASD diagnosis is broader in the DSM V (Diagnostic and Statistical Manual 2013) opposed to the DSM IV (Diagnostic and Statistical Manual, 2000). There are many stages and levels of ASD, which is determined by the individual's behaviors, social skills, engagement, and the sensory skills exhibited.

Many factors and behaviors are the focus while observing and diagnosing Autism Spectrum Disorder. Health professionals are challenged with categorizing ASD levels in individuals based on the severity of each misbehavior and lack of social skills, boundaries, proximity, as well as a variety of noncompliant behaviors. These behaviors include but are not limited to refusing to comply with directives and being withdrawn.

Listed below are behaviors an individual with ASD might display. This list may be helpful when confirming and understanding the reason for the diagnosis. All of these behaviors are known to be displayed by children with Autism Spectrum Disorder. The level varies with each individual and often depends on the challenges they face. Antecedents or triggers do not have to transpire for the behavior to occur. The behavior can be displayed in any frequency, duration, or intensity. The types of antecedents or triggers that can occur or what was observed on many occasions were; if others were making eye contact when an individual was having a challenging time, non – preferred activities or tasks which the individual doesn't want to participate because he/she doesn't have any interest, mood, distractions, and etc. Anything can be a trigger, you just have to be prepared to engage and deescalate when that individual's behaviors escalate and become uncontrollable as a result of any antecedents or triggers. Most of the time or about 40% of the time, antecedents are not known right away. It takes multiple strategies to use when encouraging the individuals to open up and self – regulate their thoughts and feelings, as well as being able to get the individual to utilize (deep breathing exercises, problem solving skills, as well as using visuals) to assist with self – calming and getting back on task. It is important to document these behaviors with (frequency = how often, duration = how long, and intensity = mild, moderate, or severe) so that everything can be tracked and documented for appropriate and efficient treatment.

When confirming your speculations, whether an individual who is not diagnosed, or in the process of being diagnosed with Autism Spectrum Disorder, below is a list of known behaviors that may confirm reasons that they may be diagnoses with ASD based on some or majority of these characteristics.

| Lack of social skills | Hoarding |
|---|---|
| Inappropriate behaviors | Head banging/Head bunting |
| Inability to use gestures | Argumentive/Defensive |
| Walking on tip toes | Tantrums/Meltdowns |
| Fidgeting | Aggression (Physical/Verbal) |

| | |
|---|---|
| Eye blinking/tremors | No eye contact |
| Compliance issues | No to Low Attention – Span |
| Nervous/paranoia | Refuses to follow instructions |
| Impulsivity | Sensory deficiencies |
| Hyperactivity | Unable to accept criticism |
| Inability to process information | Loses interest easily |

| | |
|---|---|
| Doesn't take ownership/personal responsibility | Repetitious movement |
| Fixation or preoccupation | Difficulty with transitions |
| Elopement/Escape/Avoidance | Biting |
| Grinding Teeth | Scratching/Pinching |
| Unable to accept changes | Self – injurious behaviors |
| Displaying unsafe behaviors/Fearless | Tantrums/Meltdowns |
| Inability to self–regulate thoughts and feelings | Outbursts |
| Hitting chin (feeling vibrating sensation) | Escape/Avoidance |

## Tantrums and Meltdowns

While often used interchangeably, tantrums and meltdowns are two different behaviors that ASD individuals exhibit when they are having a challenging moment. Individuals who have ASD may display these behaviors when they are having a challenging moment, are unable to express thoughts and feelings, are not allowed to use a preferred item, or are displaying attention-seeking behavior. Tantrums and meltdowns may be triggered by an individual going through different stages of a crisis. Sometimes ASD individuals have tantrums or meltdowns when they become frustrated with the inability to verbalize or self-regulate their thoughts and feelings.

*Tantrums* are behavior in which an ASD individual reacts to a specific instruction or refuses to comply with interventions or strategies. Tantrums typically last from 5 to 20 minutes. When a tantrum exceeds that timeframe, it escalates into a more severe behavior known as a *meltdown*.

*Meltdowns* last for more extended periods and often result in destructive behavior. Aggression–both physical and verbal, avoidance, and elopement are common during a meltdown. There is no set time for an individual who is experiencing a meltdown; however, they usually last from 30 minutes to several hours depending on the reason the individual is unable to self-regulate their thoughts and feelings.

During tantrums and meltdowns, it is essential to document and record the experience while observing the individual. Using a timer can be useful in tracking the duration of a tantrum or meltdown. Notes should always be taken on the reason the tantrum and/or meltdown occurred. Sometimes there will not be a trigger, but the individual is unable to handle specific situations. Documenting the frequency, duration, and intensity will allow the parent to share the information with the other members of the care team. School staff, I.E.P. (Individualized Education Plan) case managers, as well as family and/or friends must be made aware of these tantrums so appropriate and effective strategies and interventions can be implemented by all.

# Chapter 3
# **Parental Fears**
## *"You're Not Alone"*

There are parental fears when it comes to understanding the ASD diagnosis. Some caregivers may experience high levels of anxiety because they don't know how to think, what to think, or how to react. The primary concern of the parent is who will take care of their autistic child if something happens to them.

To decrease the high levels of anxiety and frustrations, caregivers must be able to accept, understand, and research the diagnosis. Learning how to transfer appropriate skills and assisting the child(ren) in adapting to his/her environment (home, community, and school) with the use of strategies and interventions will ease the caregiver's apprehension about ASD.

There are questions that may arise when the caregiver starts thinking, such as:

- Who will take care of my child if something happens to me?
- What are some things that can be setup for my child in case something happens to me?
- What can I do now?
- Who will my child reside with?
- Does my child understand their diagnosis and services they are receiving?

- How can I prepare my child?
- Will my child be able to survive without me?

Modeling and implementing effective strategies and interventions, in addition to refusing to coddle or baby the individual, can establish a solid foundation for success should someone other than the parent have to provide care in the future.

Parental involvement in the child's life is critical. The ultimate goal is to teach and prepare the child for independence by implementing and incorporating independent and realistic activities that he/she will perform on a daily basis.

## *Important Skills and Responsibilities*

Life Skills

- Cleaning, cooking, and laundry
- Hygiene, personal care, and personal grooming
- Scheduling appointments
- Daily medication intake
- Attending and participating in groups
- Community involvement/volunteering
- Community-based programs for ASD individuals
- Earning money and money management
- Finding community-based programs for exceptional children

The more the child is allowed to learn responsibility, the smoother the transition to independence will be. The parent will be relieved to witness their child's milestones. It will become a natural daily task for the child to complete tasks and/or attend events. This goes with being able to understand public transportation routes, walking routes, administering medication(s) on a daily basis, as well as being enrolled in a work or career program.

# Chapter 4
# **Needs and Wants**
## *"Differences between Needs and Wants"*

*Needs*

Individuals diagnosed with Autism Spectrum Disorder, like all individuals, require dependable, loving, welcoming, nurturing, and consistent people in their lives. Children who are on the spectrum must have stern, nurturing individuals who are trustworthy and able to develop a positive rapport while offering a structured environment.

Without consistency, ASD individuals will fall off task and will not be able to complete tasks/activities daily. Usually, when an individual on the spectrum does not have a routine or individuals are unable to provide a stable daily life, they regress or their needs are not met. When an individual regress, the caretaker or professional has to find alternate ways to assist these individuals in getting them back on track.

*Wants*

It is evident by the high levels of noncompliant behaviors displayed, ASD individuals want to be in control of everything. They feel that being in control gives them power; however, they don't understand that everything they want is not always good for them. ASD individuals do not always want to comply with instructions given. This is a result of their being in a different state of mind cognitively. The caregiver should not give ASD individuals things they want because of their extreme preoccupation and fixation.

Wants are not required. In the ASD life, a long list of needs exists that requires the attention of the caregiver. Wants are things that cannot be controlled by the caregiver, but implementing expectations are helpful. The ASD individual will learn to understand and be aware of their responsibilities and duties. If expectations are not implemented by the age of two, ASD children will have difficulties functioning in their everyday lives. They will struggle with complying to the word "no".

It is vital to understand and distinguish between needs and wants to encourage the ASD individual proper responses to authority.

There are many things that an ASD individual need in order to make progress in any environment. Some *needs* are but not limited to;

- Routine
- Consistency
- Reminders
- preferred items
- foods
- feeding times
- and etc.

By having the above mentioned needs in place with the ASD individual, these items will guide and prepare the individual to learn a routine, become familiarized with it, as well as assisting with a smoother transition.

## Picky Eaters

This may be one of the most challenging topics for discussion, when it comes to Autism Spectrum Disorder. Searching to find a variety of foods, for these individuals, can be difficult. You are not alone! Some of these individuals struggle and aren't able to process the way a certain food looks, feel, smell, or taste, which they will refuse any contact with. There are ways in which these individuals are able to learn how to adapt to specific foods or a feeding schedule when having a combination of; preferred food choices and non- preferred food choices. When creating and establishing a schedule, be sure to include, at least two regular meals (breakfast and lunch or lunch and dinner) and two snack times that are implemented. This will both; expose these individuals with the choices of non – preferred and preferred foods as well as sensory processing which they will have no choice but to taste, smell, and touch the non – preferred foods. This schedule will welcome and encourage the individual with an appropriate schedule. For example; cut up or make small portions of non – preferred and preferred food choices. Start off giving a preferred food choice and once the individual eats it, you can then give him/her the non – preferred food choice (usually a healthier item such as a fruit or vegetable). Rotate and repeat each step as much as necessary. When a schedule is changed, please make everyone aware so that all entities can be on the same page. This will decrease confusions, tantrums, and frustrated behaviors.

# Chapter 5
# How the Brain Is Known to Work
## *"Executive Functioning"*

The manner in which the individual thinks and how their brain works ultimately leads to the ASD diagnosis. Individuals with ASD have a different thought process, which can be difficult to decipher.

***Executive functioning*** is a set of abilities that allows us to involve voluntary control of our behavioral responses, which enables individuals to follow and develop plans with the use of social rules, problem-solving, and adapting to unexpected changes within one's environment.

Depending on the level and severity of an ASD individual, the brain works in a variety of ways. Some individuals are not able to process information easily, but they are encouraged to take their time and follow through the plan. A good caregiver will break down the demands into small steps. The ASD individual is able to understand the steps and complete the task.

An individual with ASD is unaware of the deficiency in their thought process. When given instructions or a specific demand, the individual will likely be off topic and ignore what is said to them. They will either do what they want to do or what they *think* they were instructed to do.

Examples of thought processes witnessed by professionals are:

1. Talking about three or more topics in one sentence. The individual is unable to stick to the same topic and may require some prompts so they can understand and remember what they were talking about or need to focus on.
2. Losing focus, zoning out, and not being able to remain on task. These individuals are unable to process information appropriately. They may be limited to directives of no more than two steps.
3. Transitions are challenging. They struggle to comply with instructions due to their lack of focus. Elopement can occur at this time being that it is unstructured and the ASD individual assume that they can wander off, due to the lack of focus exhibited.

**Different Levels of ASD**

The ASD diagnosis has so many levels that there are unknown types that have yet to be recognized, found, or recorded. The previous Diagnostic and Statistical Manual, which was volume IV (4), outlined the ASD diagnosis. The updated DSM V (2013) had more detail than its predecessor. The DSM V has an entire section on the ASD diagnosis, including the additional diagnoses that can be combined with it, such as ADHD (Attention Deficit Hyperactive Disorder), IDD (Intellectual Development Disorder), Developmental Delay, ODD (Oppositional Defiant Disorder), PTSD (Posttraumatic Stress Disorder), etc. The multiple categories include behaviors and characteristics based on the factors experienced by the ASD individual.

The DSM is updated approximately every five years. Mental illness evolves each day. When the DSM VI is released, it is expected to contain additional behaviors under each category, assisting clinicians in correctly diagnosing the ASD individual.

Working with the ASD population for eleven years has enhanced and increased my knowledge. I have learned to understand and assign each of my clients a category based on his/her behavior, development and milestones, and concerns. After about seven years as a Licensed Behavioral Specialist, the ASD diagnosis received in 2017 by my two-year-old son, Tyler, made it personal. Tyler was diagnosed with ASD and ADHD because of the lack of sensory he displayed, as well as the severe hyperactive behaviors that he exhibited.

As a mother, I was very observant and aware of the different behaviors that were displayed. I documented milestones to see if Tyler was meeting them and if he fell in normal ranges. As a professional, I knew I was unable to diagnose my own child. It is easy to overlook important things rather than making an accurate diagnosis. I also did not want to become fixated on the behaviors that I observed my son display. Tyler had sensory deficiencies, and he would become preoccupied with ceiling fans and the lights. He would stare at them and follow them for extended periods (approximately 10–15 minutes) and become excited while doing so.

I also noticed him doing the following things:
- Spitting
- Running around
- Stimming/Clapping hands
- Different repetitious movements and behaviors
- Tip-toeing
- Climbing and displaying unsafe behaviors
- Noncompliance
- Hoarding (kept multiple objects in each hand at once). For instance, if Tyler wanted to pick something up off the floor that he wanted, he would pick it up while holding multiple objects in his hands.

Despite these behaviors, Tyler's milestones fell within normal ranges. He lifted his head at three months old, sat up at six months old, rolled over at six months old, crawled between seven to eight months old, walked at eleven months old, and fed himself at one year old. These were encouraged because of the expectations that were given as well as his levels of development that he was approaching, mastered, as well as met.

# Diagram of ASD Brain Development

Referenced: Michelson Medical Research Foundation / Groundwork / Autism Breakthrough / Autism and the Brain

# Autism and the brain

*The areas of the brain affected by autism, which stems from abnormal brain development:*

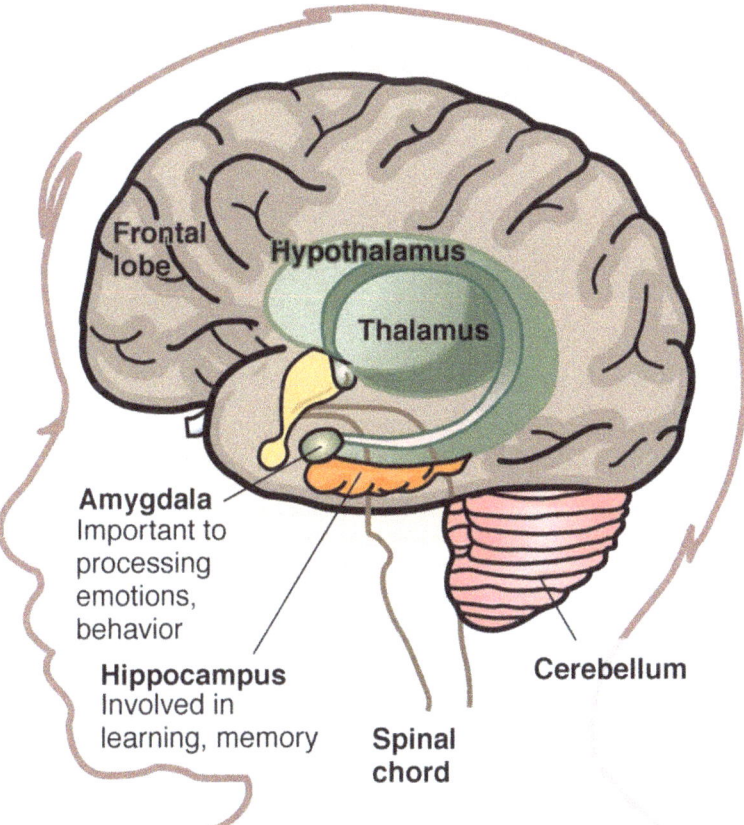

**Amygdala**
Important to processing emotions, behavior

**Hippocampus**
Involved in learning, memory

**Spinal chord**

**Cerebellum**

### Affect on brain cells (neurons)
- Cells are smaller, more densely packed in certain areas
- Have shorter, less developed branches

Source: The Journal of NIH Research

© 2012 MCT

ASD individuals think and react differently because of the way their brain functions. It is challenging for an individual to think and react to a typical individual who does not fall within normal ranges of the thought process. The way the brain functions with ASD results in the individual lacking social skills and communication. Sometimes the lack of social skills can interfere with these individuals cognitive processing thinking which is when he/she may start displaying frustrated and overwhelmed behaviors, because of the inability to self – regulate.

*Understanding Communication Issues*

- Verbal
- Nonverbal
- Lack of Speech
- Gestures
- Visuals and Other PECS (Picture Exchange Communication) Items
- Limited Speech
- Sign Language

*Sensory Issues*

- Sensitive to loud sounds, also known as "Sound Sensitive"
- Sensitive to lights (too bright, too dark), also known as "Light Sensitive"
- Sensitive to temperatures (too hot or too cold)
- Overstimulated by technology

- Overstimulated by the amount of people in their area
- Proximity and Boundaries
- Doesn't like large groups

***Behaviors***

- Elopement or wandering
- Escape/Avoidance
- Frustrations and overwhelming
- Self – injurious
- Head bunts others
- Scratches self and/or others
- Physically aggressive towards others
- Destructive
- Verbally aggressive

# Chapter 6
# <u>Important Steps to Take</u>
*"Things to Do"*

Many things should be taken into consideration after receiving a child's ASD (Autism Spectrum Disorder) diagnosis. The procedure that needs to be followed differs depending on the state of residency. Each state will have specific guidelines and procedures to get the child proper services after diagnosis. Remaining calm and researching the diagnosis will be beneficial to the parent or caregiver. The most up-to-date information will be obtained from other parents, support groups, social media groups, and developmental pediatricians. For best results, take time to research and ask questions, and create a resource guide for reference and to help others who may have questions or need assistance.

The milestones pediatricians monitor during well checkups are essential. Be sure to provide accurate information so that the child's history is recorded correctly. Pediatricians will track the child by having a parent and/or professional complete a questionnaire about milestones for sitting up, crawling, walking, talking, etc. If the pediatrician has any concerns, they will recommend E.I. (Early Interventions) services for infants and toddlers from 0–3 years of age. If the child is 3–5 years of age, Preschool Intervention Services from an Intermediate Unit will be recommended. the school district will evaluate a child who has not been diagnosed by the start of kindergarten. An assessment will be administered to see what classroom environment is appropriate for the child and which services would be beneficial.

Sometimes parents become too preoccupied and fixated on their child's developmental stages and milestones. It is important to remember that every child is different, and children should not be compared to each other. Every child develops differently.

Upon noticing repetitious behaviors, such as aggression, defiance, noncompliance, inability to process, staring or zoning out, becoming fixated on specific objects or things, parents should seek professional assistance. Any sensory preoccupations, such as flapping, clapping, stemming, fixations with particular textures, stimulation, or repetitious movements, require evaluation. The evaluations will indicate whether the child is eligible to receive an ISFP (Individualized Service Family Plan) or I.E.P. (Individualized Education Plan) for appropriate services.

The outcome of the child's intake and assessments will be outlined in the I.S.F.P. or I.E.P. and will determine the types of services the child will receive. A variety of services are available, including speech and language therapy, physical therapy, occupational therapy, and special education services.

Once the I.S.F.P. or I.E.P. is completed, an I.E.P. meeting will be scheduled to discuss the assessment results and services that the child will receive. The individuals in attendance at the I.E.P. meeting are teachers, speech, occupational, and physical therapists, caretakers, parents, guardians, school's behavior support, wraparound, and a school district representative.

The I.E.P. is reviewed to update and validate the effective and appropriate interventions and strategies used. Measurable goals will be outlined to track the interventions, objectives, and outcomes. Goals are adjusted during this meeting if the child has exceeded a specific target. New goals are documented, and any changes to the interventions of previous goals are agreed upon and notated. An example of a measurable goal is: Child will exhibit compliant behaviors within 4 out of 6 instances with the use of 3-4 prompts. The numbers may be too tense or not tense enough for the child; therefore, adjustments may be appropriate and effective for the child. The I.F.S.P./I.E.P. is a law-abiding document that agrees to implement strategies and focus on the goals outlined through the text.

After the goals are reviewed, all parties will provide their input on whether the child is progressing or regressing in the current placement. Any required revisions are discussed and documented. The N.O.R.E.P. (Notice of Recommendation Education Placement) will be addressed as the I.E.P. meeting is concluding. The N.O.R.E.P. is the current placement in which the child is currently enrolled. The caretaker has the right to agree or disagree with the current placement. After reviewing the decision presented at the I.E.P. meeting, the caregiver is required to check off either box and sign at the very bottom of the sheet. When the caregiver checks "DISAGREE" with the current placement that the child is in, a reason for disagreement must be written. A caregiver who ignores or refuses to write in the space provided has ten days before their child is moved from current placement and is unable to receive appropriate services. If the caregiver disagrees, the child's school district also only gets ten days to respond or think of alternate strategies or curriculum for the child. Sometimes there are waiting lists and a very long process for approved private schools because of the state's funding.

The I.E.P. (Individualized Education Plan) is a law-abiding document that school districts create to provide services to an individual who requires additional assistance or specialized placement geared to their needs. Once the I.E.P. process is complete and all documents executed, it is considered approved.

Once the I.E.P. is completed, the eligible service will be scheduled. Speech and language, occupational therapy, or physical therapy are usually scheduled on a weekly or 6-day cycle, depending on the child's school district. These services also occur for thirty minutes per session. If there is a concern in more than one area, the sessions can be combined. The specialists collaborate to identify problems in specific areas that require extra attention.

Even though the individual may receive speech and language, occupational therapy, and physical therapy in the school environment, the caretaker is encouraged to continue reinforcing the skills at home. This continuation of care will strengthen the child's deficiencies and establish a structured routine across settings. (Please see ideas and lists in Chapter 8.)

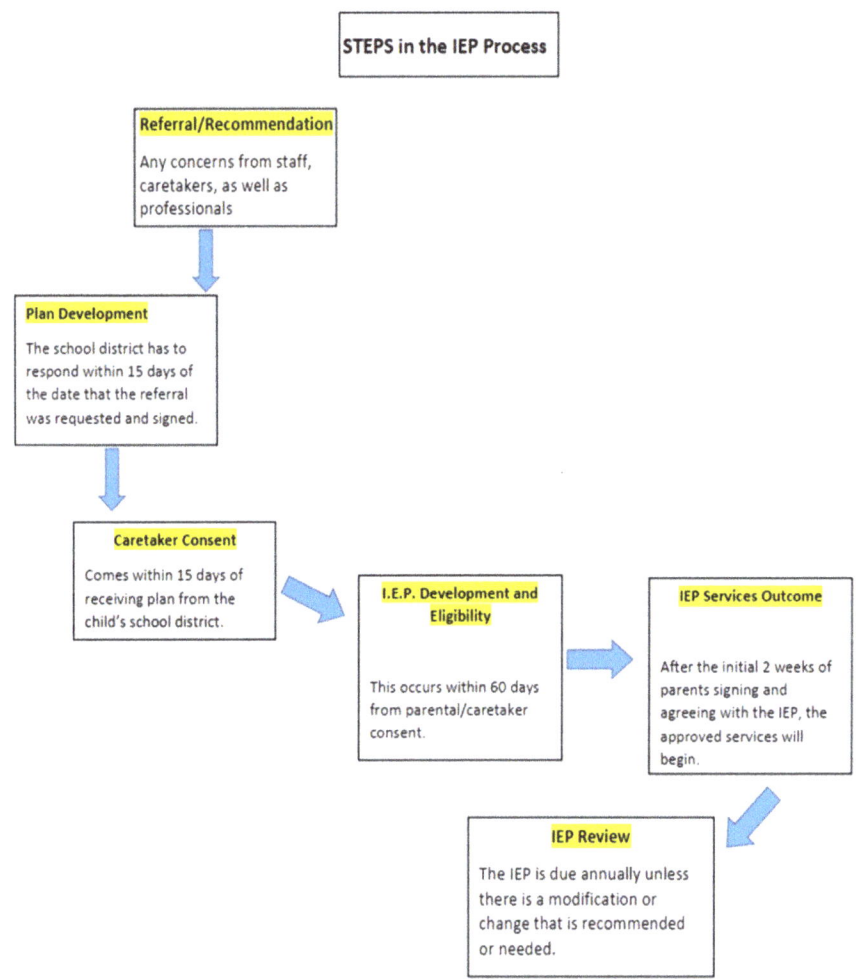

## Developmental Pediatrician

Children who are diagnosed with Autism Spectrum Disorder should be followed by a developmental pediatrician. A developmental pediatrician is a licensed practitioner who specializes in areas of autism. Sometimes there is a waiting list, but no matter how long it takes, the caregiver should keep following up with the facility, completing all requested questionnaires and assessments until the child is taken off the waiting list and given an appointment. The caregiver should annually research the best developmental pediatricians to ensure their child is receiving the best care available.

Based on the diagnoses the child has been given, the developmental pediatrician may request MRI, EEG, or genetics testing to see if there are any neurological impairments or deficiencies. Identifying these deficiencies will allow the child to receive additional services. The developmental pediatrician usually re-evaluates the child once a year unless there are concerns or medical impairments that require continuous visits.

The staff members, such as; medical assistant, social worker, intake coordinator, or the physician will furnish the parent or guardian with helpful resources relevant to their child's diagnosis. They may also find funding for the child to receive weighted blankets, weighted vests, compression vests, sensory items, or other supplies that will help decrease the child's hyperactive, impulsive, noncompliant, and aggressive behaviors.

**Joining Support Groups**

Valuable resources will come from other parents who have successfully implemented plans for their autistic children. Sharing information helps everyone on the journey with an autistic child. It is imperative to join social media pages, such as Facebook, Instagram, and Twitter, as well as local groups that provide assistance.

After joining these groups, parents and professionals will implement effective strategies and skills that may work for their children. As a mother and a licensed professional, I advise parents to research the diagnosis, reach out to others, make connections, bridge gaps, and build relationships. Sharing information and assisting others with new information helps everyone with their journey.

**Data and Assessments**

Discovering antecedents or triggers, replacement strategies, current concerning behaviors, and academic deficiencies will help the caregiver determine the most effective tool to track this data.

There are many different tools and assessments used in tracking data. The appropriate tool to use depends on the concerns and needs. The different types of assessments usually used to track concerning behaviors are F.B.A., (Functional Behavioral Assessment), B.I.P. (Behavior Intervention Plan), CANS (Child and Adolescent Needs Strengths), ASSQ (Autism Spectrum Screening Questionnaire), GARS (Gilliam Autism Rating Scale), ATEC (Autism Treatment Evaluation Checklist), and ASRS (Autism Spectrum Rating Scales. The preferred tool varies depending on the state, level of autism, environment, and age appropriateness.

If the ASD individual is presenting problems, the school district may have a meeting or telephone conference with the parent to get the consent and permission necessary to complete a specific assessment or data tracker. Caretaker is responsible to sign documents furnished and sent home so that appropriate assessments and tests can be administered. Without the signature, the ASD individual will not begin receiving services.

**Functional Behavior Assessment or F.B.A.**

A Functional Behavioral Assessment (F.B.A.) determines the reasons an individual is displaying certain behaviors. This tool uses a variety of data and techniques to help understand the inappropriate behaviors that the individual is exhibiting. In an F.B.A., specific things are reviewed that may be contributing to the individual's frustration with learning, excluding the individual's academic factors.

Learning and understanding the mechanics of an F.B.A. increases awareness of what's considered inappropriate and alternate strategies to change the behaviors displayed. The F.B.A. is broken down into direct and indirect assessments, depending on each individual's needs.

**Direct**

Direct is a comprehensive assessment that focuses on when the target behavior becomes severe by listing the intensity, frequency, and duration of each behavior patterns displayed. The different factors examined when completing a direct F.B.A. are:

- Defining target behaviors
- Collecting data
- Planning interventions and strategies to implement with the individual
- Effective plan of action

## Indirect

An indirect assessment is completed under the F.B.A. depending on the time when behaviors require immediate attention and action. This type of evaluation involves fewer individuals so that multiple professionals in one room will not overstimulate the ASD individual. The important factors examined when completing an indirect F.B.A. are:

- No more than three professionals are consulted
- Implements simple verbal or written feedback
- Focuses on the history or interviews of professionals and parents about behaviors presented in each category

The type of F.B.A. assessment utilized varies based on the ASD individual's needs. F.B.A. usually focuses on the environment in which the individual is currently being observed in, whether it being the home, school, or community setting. Sometimes the environment may have an impact on an individual's behaviors, which is the reason why this assessment is combined; across environments (home, school and community) and collaborate the information for appropriate goals to work on.

## Behavior Intervention Plan or B.I.P.

A Behavior Intervention Plan or B.I.P. is effective when I.E.P. goals are outlined. This broadens the layout of the I.E.P. plan and better implements and assists with challenging and difficult behaviors. The B.I.P. exhibits any academics in the plan; however, positive behavioral interventions, strategies, and support are the focus. This plan also includes skills and alternate behavioral strategies that more appropriately meet the individual's needs.

The B.I.P. contains feedback or findings from the F.B.A., and a variety of things included in this plan are crucial in collecting data. The data that is required to be a part of the B.I.P. include:

- A detailed description of the problem that is occurring
- Hypothesis as to why these specific behaviors occur
- Problematic behaviors and their antecedents or triggers
- Positive supports, strategies, and interventions, as well as effective visuals

Once the F.B.A. or B.I.P. is finalized, a meeting is scheduled with the caretaker(s), school staff, as well as other vital individuals to discuss the findings and recommendations. After review, the plan is added to the I.E.P. If a new placement is recommended, a N.O.R.E.P. is signed by the caretaker if they agree. If the caretaker disagrees, they have the option not to sign and request a different placement.

**Assessments and Rating Scales**

Which assessment to use is determined by the age concerns arise with the child's development and milestones. Many tools can be used to assess the child's needs as early as infancy when limited social skills are exhibited. Assessments are initiated with concerns from the individual's current placement, pediatrician, or parent and then followed-up with questionnaires, family history, observable behaviors, and other important information needed to assist with the process for receiving appropriate services for the individual.

**Autism Treatment Evaluation Checklist (ATEC)**

ATEC is an assessment used both professionally and personally on ASD individuals for the past seven years. This tool, which was developed by Bernard Rimland and Stephen Edelson with the Autism Research Institute, was initially geared towards individuals with an efficient way of screening children between the ages of five and twelve years old.

Many support the ATEC and believe this tool is valid and reliable. The ATEC is also divided into four different subscales detailing whether or not a child is making progress or regressing with their current treatment. The subscales consist of measurements of behavior, cognitive awareness, and communication with other standardized measures of the same characteristics. There are four sections that the ATEC focuses on when scoring each individual. These sections are:

- Speech/Language and Communication
- Sociability
- Sensory/Cognitive Behaviors
- Health/Physical Behavior

It is important to have the caretaker, staff, and anyone else who plays a vital role in the child's life to complete an ATEC. A professional will score each ATEC received to determine the results of the assessment. The ATEC is scored using the www.autism.com/atec website. *(Bernard Rimland, Ph.D. & Stephen M. Edelson, Ph.D.)* After all the input is submitted, the site provides a number score, enabling professionals to ascertain the individual's level and progression or regression in comparison to the previous scores. The higher the score of the ATEC, the more severe the level of ASD the individual is categorized.

## Behavioral Health (wraparound services) BHRS which is now IBHS

Behavioral Health is transitioning to Intensive Behavioral Health Services (IBHS) in the near future. This change is occurring to merge behavioral health, ABA, and other services that are a medical necessity for ASD individuals.

Wraparound services is an involuntary service that is chosen by the caretaker. They may feel like their child, who is between the ages of two and twenty years old, requires additional help to learn how to cope and comply with daily life activities at home, school, or community events. Individuals must meet certain criteria to be eligible for wraparound services. There are steps the caretaker must take for their child to receive wraparound services. After reviewing the outcome of the initial evaluation or extended assessment, a licensed professional will make recommendations. These steps include:

- Extended assessment
- Findings and recommendations of the extended assessment
- Wraparound services recommendation

Using the results of the extended assessment, a licensed professional will determine the individual's eligibility for wraparound services. These individuals will receive a BSC

(Behavior Specialist Consultant) or LBS (Licensed Behavior Specialist), MT (Mobile Therapist), and/or TSS (Therapeutic Staff Support) Worker. The number of hours increases with the increased need of the individual. The BSC/LBS is the individual who supervises the individual's case and creates the treatment plan. To ensure everyone is on the same page, the plan must be executed by the individual's entire care team. The responsibilities and duties for each wraparound role are detailed below.

## Licensed Behavioral Specialist (LBS)/Behavior Specialist Consultant (BSC)

A Behavioral Specialist Consultant (BSC) supervises each of their clients. The responsibilities of the BSC include the collection of data and creating an initial treatment plan that consists of goals, objectives, interventions, and strategies, as well as a description of the roles of each person working the case. A behavior specialist also coordinates Functional Behavioral Assessments and Behavior Intervention Plan, working closely with the family and school. The behavior specialist also outlines appropriate skills to be used by the family, team, and school, enabling the client to learn expectations and responsibilities.

Behavioral Specialist Consultants (BSC) are required to become licensed with the State Board of Medicine to work with children diagnosed with ASD. Once the BSC becomes licensed, it is a requirement for them to complete at least eight continuing education hours annually through the ABA Training or Applied Behavior Analysis.

The LBS or BSC will create behavior programs, visuals, and other positive reinforcement rewards systems. These systems have proven to be effective and efficient. ASD individuals can relate well to things visually and can better understand expectations with these systems. The BSC/LBS observes the individual in an environment, documents and tracks specific problematic behaviors, teaches skills to adults who are present during sessions, and ensures the use of appropriate strategies. Redirections, prompts, counting backward, planned ignoring, and taking breaks are examples of the strategies usually implemented in sessions with the individual.

Depending on the goals or severity of the client's concerning behaviors, additional strategies, such as deep breathing exercises and problem-solving thinking strategies, may be used to de-escalate and assist the client with understanding.

**Mobile Therapist (MT)**

A mobile therapist, also known as an MT, is not a required service. All individuals are not eligible for an MT. They must be recommended by a licensed professional. Mobile therapists are clinicians with a master's degree who provide in-home or community services in a therapeutic environment. Usually, a mobile therapist is only able to offer clinical services in the school environment if they are the only clinician on the case.

A mobile therapist is supervised by a BSC/LBS and follows all interventions and responsibilities listed in the treatment plan. The treatment plan is created for each individual and details specific goals, objectives, interventions, and strategies deemed effective and appropriate.

Mobile therapists are responsible for providing individual and family counseling, implementing and utilizing therapeutic strategies, and identifying problematic thoughts or behavior. These clinicians also use a variety of therapies, including Play, Cognitive Behavioral, Drug and Alcohol, Group, Dialectical Behavioral, and Emotion-Focused Therapy. Because of the smaller environment and individualized sessions, the clinician is able to use a wide variety of therapies. Mobile therapists can provide insight on what is happening by implementing strategies, such as redirection, verbal cues, role-playing, prompting, planned ignoring, deep breathing exercises, and individual-based strategies, depending on the individual's needs. Mobile therapists also assist with the development of a child's strengths, which can increase the therapeutic effectiveness of family dynamics. In addition, the therapist builds a relationship with the individual and their family and implements child-centered therapy, which helps the individual relate to therapy on a personal level and allows the clinician to focus on the individual's needs more therapeutically. If there needs to be changes or revisions to the treatment plan, the mobile therapist will discuss them with the Behavior Specialist Consultant.

**Therapeutic Staff Support (TSS Worker)**

Therapeutic Staff Support Worker works one-on-one with an individual for a prescribed number of hours. The individual's eligibility is based on their assessments, history, and current behavior. Sometimes it is challenging for an individual to receive a TSS Worker. The types of TSS Worker eligible behaviors are unsafe, off task, requires continuous strategies to be enforced, physical aggression, zero to low attention span, elopement and wandering, and other behaviors that impede academics, emotional, physical, and daily life.

There are two types of TSS services. Some certifications are required when working with ASD children. TSS services are offered in the home, community, and school environments. Depending on the needs of the individual, he/she may be approved for both home and school hours.

The role of the TSS Worker is to support caretakers, school staff, and the clinical team by recommending and demonstrating skills and strategies to assist the ASD individual. TSS Workers are assigned to at-risk children who are unsafe, challenging, and struggle to remain calm and focused.

TSS Workers implement the following interventions:

- Redirections and prompts
- Close proximity and encourage staying within personal boundaries
- Observing and tracking data (usually a data sheet is furnished by BSC) to track behaviors
- Planned ignoring (attention-seeking behaviors)
- Breathing exercises
- Frequency, intensity, and duration of each concerned behavior the individual displays

A TSS Worker is part of the therapeutic team that makes a positive impact on the clients who they are assigned. TSS Workers learn skills from the BSC/LBS and utilize these skills to assist the ASD individuals.

## Medication (Agree, Opposed, and When)

The most appropriate way to deal with a child who is diagnosed with any special needs, especially Autism, is controversial. The topic has been debated for over twenty-five years. Each caretaker should research their options and talk with the wraparound team about the pros and cons of medication.

Parents are often concerned about when they should begin administering medication, and they fear others are coercing their child to take them. As a parent of a ASD child, I suggest caretakers consider medication if alternative strategies have not worked and they notice the child displaying the following behaviors:

- No to low attention span
- Moderate to severe hyperactive, impulsive, or anxious behaviors
- Unable to comply with strategies and directives that are given
- Appearing to have mood changes or racing thoughts
- Not able to stay focused, on task, and zones out a lot
- Unable to complete academic assessments or other schoolwork

If alternate strategies and interventions have been unsuccessful and the caretaker is contacted continuously regarding the behavior, the child would be referred for psychiatric services and prescribed medication.

Caretakers should not listen to others about what medications work or compare the experiences of other children or family members with their child's situation. Everyone is different and reacts to medications differently. It is best to consult a licensed psychiatrist who will provide parents with accurate information relevant to their child's condition and prescribe effective medication for them.

Parents should be prepared to try more than one medication. Adjustments may need to be made four or more times to find the appropriate medication and the most effective dosage to regulate a child's daily life and routine. It is important not to get frustrated. The parent has to sign a consent form permitting the school's nurse to administer medication at specified times during the school day. No child should be taken off of any of his/her prescribed medication without the recommendation of a psychiatrist. Discontinuing a child's medication on weekends, holidays, or to give them a break can be harmful for the child. This decision will adversely affect a child for a few days when they return to their educational setting.

Professionally speaking, there are things to consider when consulting a licensed psychiatrist regarding their strategies, interventions, hands-on experience, and appropriate wraparound services to assist with the child's behavioral needs. A professional working with ASD children will review the following things prior to prescribing medications:

- The child's needs
- Measurable goals and objectives with schools and/or wraparound team
- An extended assessment for approved wraparound services (if the individual isn't currently receiving services)
- Consequences being enforced and the structure of the home environment to understand the expectations and boundaries in place for the individual
- Whether or not the individual is receiving telephone or emails home every day

If the caretaker has exhausted all alternative options and the child has continued to display inappropriate, unsafe, off task, hyperactive, impulsive, anxious, defiant and noncompliant behaviors, psychiatric services should be consulted.

A child struggling with ongoing symptoms usually requires psychiatric intervention. While some children are able to cope, comply, and engage in life without medication, they do not display moderate to severe behavior concerns. There are also some children who may outgrow these behaviors, but the majority will not, and the behavior will become worse as the child ages.

**Scenario:** A child displaying all the above behaviors, whether exhibited intentionally or unintentionally, is constantly challenged and struggles with everyday life. In a class setting, the child may walk around, become destructive, and be aggressive towards peers and teachers. This individual may not be able to sit still because of the racing and inappropriate thoughts that are confusing them. They will be unable to understand the strategies implemented. Instead, they may continuously run around, trying to escape reality while disrupting the classroom. The lessons are not comprehended despite the strategies implemented and additional support. The child is still struggling to complete the assignments given. As a result, frustration arises, and the ASD individual shuts down and begins displaying off-task behaviors that interfere with everyone's ability to learn. Their inability to understand and mood changes are detrimental to the learning environment. The scenario is confusing for everyone involved. It's a small glimpse into the mind of an ASD individual. The confusion is compounded by combine diagnoses such as ASD with ADHD, ASD with ODD, ASD with PTSD, etc. These individuals think differently and are challenged daily. Psychiatric recommendations would be beneficial in decreasing disorderly behavior and mood changes and establishing a routine.

**Intelligence Quotient (IQ) and Gifted**

Intelligence Quotient tests are usually administered in an I.E.P. for all children, especially with ASD individuals, to test their brain functions. These assessments are given not only to determine the level of brain functionality from a medical perspective but also to learn what age the brain is functioning in to gauge eligibility and appropriateness of available services. IQ is calculated by dividing a person's mental age by chronological age and then multiplying by 100. This information is gathered using the child's level of performance on the IQ test. The score reflects where the individual falls in comparison with others in their age group.

## *The range of IQ's for ASD children*

An ASD individual whose range of IQ is 115 or higher is considered High Functioning or gifted. These individuals usually excel academically, socially, and emotionally. The majority of individuals may have an I.E.P. for the Gifted Program and can receive appropriate services.

Individuals with an IQ of less than 70 will most likely fall into the moderate to severe levels of ASD, while individuals who have an IQ of 70-84 suffer from a mild degree of ASD typically. The outcome of the IQ indicates the child's eligibility for services. Parents may have to advocate for the child. Requests for the administration of any assessment must be submitted in writing to the principal, school district, teachers, or special education supervisors. The caregiver's request should include a detailed reason why they feel the child needs to be evaluated.

## ASD Individuals Approaching Adulthood

Advocacy for a child does not stop at age seventeen. Just because the child is approaching adulthood does not mean they no longer need services. There are still a variety of services that they will continue to receive or services in which they can enroll before graduating. Most of these individuals are eligible to graduate when they are 21-years-old, which is more effective with learning life skills and community preparedness.

As the individual approaches the age of eighteen, they should begin the process of applying for OVR (Office of Vocational Rehabilitation), IDS (Intellectual Disability Services), and various other resources that the school's guidance counselor, teacher, or social worker will recommend. Once the individual reaches the age of eighteen, he/she can apply for SSI (Social Security), register to vote, and if this individual is a male, he is required to register for the Selective Services, especially when applying for Social Security.

**Guardianship**

When the ASD individuals become young adults, they may not be able to understand a lot of their new responsibilities and may struggle with the real world around them. Caretakers can apply for guardianship, giving them the right to make decisions for their child if they feel the child is not mentally capable of advocating for themselves. This keeps the child from being held responsible for any involuntary or uncontrollable actions. Guardianship documents are legal documents that must be filed by a lawyer to be official.

# Important Steps to Take For Each Age Level

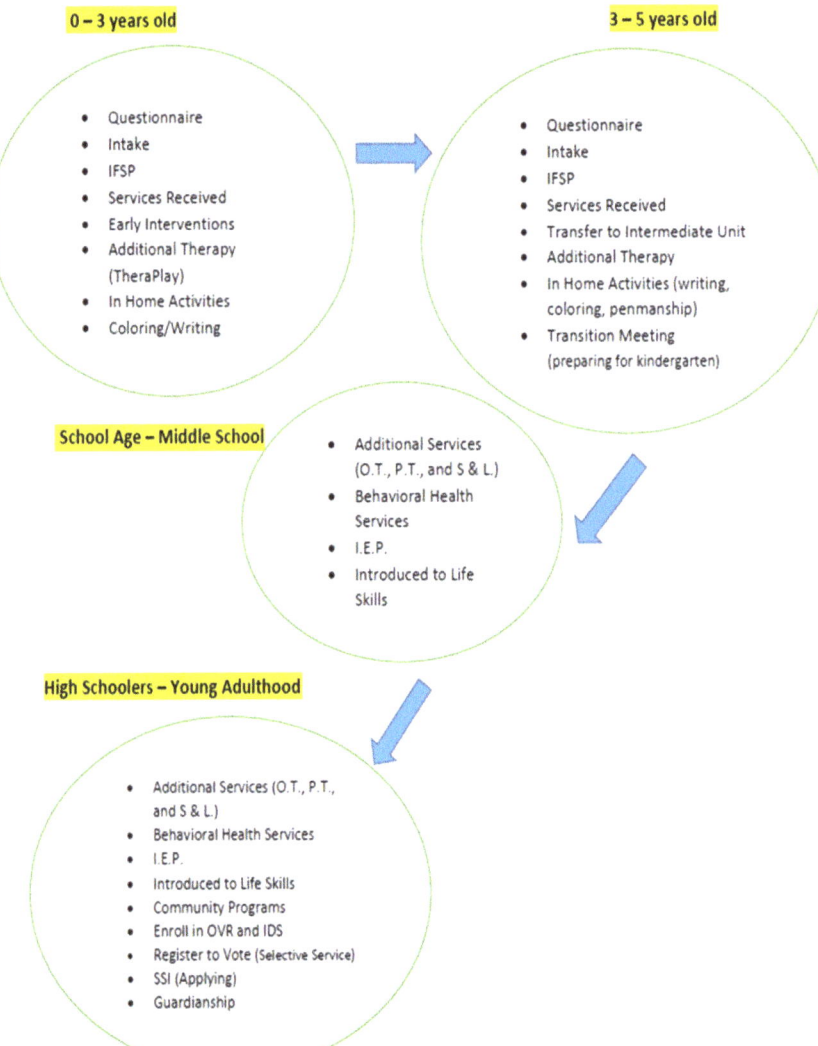

## Parental Organization "BINDER"

Requiring expectations from an Exceptional individual to meet, on a daily basis is realistic, however there are multiple strategies and interventions that are used. ASD individuals require organization and others who engage and interact with them, on a daily basis to be organized as well.

Having a Binder for the individual is very important. You will become the most organized advocate for this individual by placing; IEP's, NOREP's, BIP's, Assessments, Behavior Plans and Charts, Conferences, and etc. in this binder. Please use dividers, binders and folders to separate everything so when you need to reference or confirm specific items, it is easy to identify and find. Purchasing a 3" or Larger and start from there. Do not throw anything away because you may need it. This is helpful when you want to view the individual's files for resources that were discussed, but needed the additional information to make contacts for specific programs and services that the individual is eligible for.

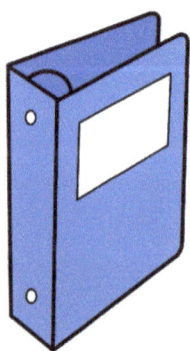

*The more organized you are, the less frustrated and high anxiety you will exhibit.*

# Chapter 7
# Strategies and Interventions
*"Which Are Most Effective and Utilized?"*

**Boundaries and Proximity**

Boundaries and proximity are significant with the ASD child. These individuals must be taught to understand and respect the personal spaces of others. Individuals with Autistic Spectrum Disorder sometimes cross acceptable boundaries because of excitement or repetitious movements that they display.

Modeling is an effective strategy and intervention used to help ASD individuals understand the boundaries set by others. One strategy consists of putting their arm out in front of them to demonstrate their limits. While their arm is extended, it should be explained that there should be at least two inches of space between them and the individual they are encountering. The proximity and boundaries rule will have to be continuously repeated throughout the child's treatment so it can be embedded in their mind.

**Redirection**

Redirection is the most effective strategy used in the treatment of the ASD child. This strategy sends a constant reminder to the child, reinforcing limits. Redirection is also implemented and utilized to enforce rules and expectations. These children are usually off task, unfocused, and not able to understand safety or rules. When the child is redirected, there is eye contact made, and the behavior is either stopped or the child will slowly refrain from displaying it.

## Prompting

Prompting is another important strategy and intervention used with a child who has special needs. In children diagnosed with ASD, they struggle with thought processing, and some are unable to complete more than two-step directives. Prompting is used when the child is completing a step and requires assistance along the way. When this child struggles, one or two-word verbal cues are given to assist the child with finishing the directive.

## Planned Ignoring

Planned ignoring is very important to attention-seeking children. These children often exhibit a variety of behaviors, including severe tantrums and meltdowns, until the caretaker, educator, or professional responds. While planned ignoring can be effective at times, some incidents require an immediate response to the attention-seeking behaviors, such as self-injurious behaviors or behaviors that affect others.

## Positive Reinforcement

Positive reinforcement is an excellent strategy to use when the child requires confirmation that they are exhibiting appropriate behavior. Positive reinforcement can also be useful when a child is off task and to help them comply with directives. The child is inspired to make appropriate choices with positive reinforcement, which will keep them from regressing.

In the ABA World, positive reinforcement encourages the child to comply and understand expectations, with reminders every 3-10 minutes depending on the severity of the behaviors exhibited.

## Verbal Praise

Verbal praise motivates the child toward better choices. This is effective and appropriate for kids who respond well to praise. The consistent and positive reminders that they are making the right choices helps them focus on expectations and guides the child while instilling appropriate boundaries.

## De-escalating and Deep Breathing Exercises

When the ASD child has reached a severe point of escalation, de-escalation can take a very long time. Depending on the level of noncompliant behaviors, it can take the appropriate strategies from ten minutes to over an hour to calm the child.

Helping an escalated child is challenging. Sometimes they are not aware of the noncompliant and defiant behaviors that have transpired. They struggle and are not able to communicate their wants and needs. The ASD individual requires assurance and trust during this de-escalation process. First, the caregiver should speak a few words to help the child understand they are safe. After establishing that trust, the caregiver must use strategies to ensure the child complies with appropriate behavior.

During the de-escalation process, asking the child why and what the reasons are for the escalation may be a helpful strategy. It will require a lot of prompting and patience since the child is unable to express his or her thoughts and feelings.

Being aware of the reason the child is exhibiting these behaviors is helpful when offering alternative options and seeking the best de-escalation strategy.

For example, Jeff, **FIRST,** you have to listen and follow directions, and **"THEN"** you can have some iPad time (or another preferred activity in which the child usually engages).

The caretaker may have to repeat the directive or place the item in their hand when implementing this strategy. The child will be aware of what steps to follow to receive the preferred item he or she is requesting. The adult has to be approachable and maintain a non-threatening demeanor while using child-friendly terms.

If the child is experiencing a tantrum, meltdown, or displaying attention-seeking behavior, strategies – such as planned ignoring – should be utilized. The child will see that misbehavior will not be encouraged or rewarded. It may take time, and the parents may have to walk away. The child is watching to see if the caregiver is going to comply with their demands. Deep breathing exercises are imperative during this time. The child can take deep breaths while counting to five. About ten deep breaths should be taken to help the child become calm. If the child is not physically aggressive, place a paper towel wet with cold water on the child's forehead. While holding the paper towel on the child's forehead, compressions can be applied. This strategy will decrease their impulsive, aggressive, and hyperactive behaviors. The change in body temperature will assist with calming the child. When the child regains full control and can comprehend a conversation, the caregiver should immediately explain the misbehaviors that were displayed and how the situation should be handled in the future.

## Coping Items to Use

Many items can be incorporated in a child's daily life, whether in a home, school, or community environment. The child's reaction will determine the effectiveness of the strategies used.

Some children have issues with physical aggression, verbal aggression, crossing boundaries, hyperactive and impulsive behaviors, off-task and unfocused behaviors, and their attention span. Certain objects are useful for helping calm the ASD child, enabling them to be more focused and on task.

Some of these items are:
- Cushioned Chair or Cushion for Chair
- Wedge for Chair
- Stress Ball
- Yoga Ball
- Fidget Cubes
- Manipulatives (blocks and puzzles)
- Chew Toy
- Head Phones (block out distractions and loud noises)
- Weighted Vest/Weighted Blanket
- Sensory Swing

It may also be helpful to use a timer to assist the individual's understanding of transitions, respecting personal boundaries, and time limits. The timer usually helps to prepare the child with the next steps to follow or to encourage some independence and responsibility.

# Chapter 8
## Helpful Programs/Services
*"Networking and Researching"*

Many assistance programs have been established or are being created due to the increase in children being diagnosed with ASD, some as young as age two. Annually, pediatricians give parents a questionnaire to complete detailing their child's milestones and developments based on their observations.

Sometimes, pediatricians are not able to correctly diagnose a child, but they may notice social, emotional, or physical deficiencies or delays and recommend Early Intervention for children up to three years of age or Preschool Intervention for children ages three to five. The pediatrician may then refer other specialists for a complete psychological evaluation to determine the child's diagnosis or eligibility for additional services.

If the specialist is concerned and schedules the child for a follow-up appointment, the parent should consider contacting a local hospital that specializes in ASD/Developmental Delay Children. Partnering with such a facility allows the child to be tracked yearly by professionals who are familiar with the trends of the disorder. This Development Pediatrician will possibly request an MRI, EKG, genetic testing, etc. Depending on the outcome of the intake, as well as the history and background of the child, additional testing may be administered. Parents should not get discouraged. The waitlist for an appointment can be anywhere from six months to three years, depending on the area of residence. It is best to complete the questionnaire, make a copy, and submit it. If no response or correspondence has been received in six months, give them a call to confirm they received the forms and inquire about the estimated time for the child's case to be reviewed.

## Different Establishments Who Have Sensory Areas and Days for ASD Kids

### (Montgomery County)

Children on the ASD Spectrum have challenges with the community environment, also known as the outside world. It is challenging for many of these children to enjoy the community environment because they exhibit different behaviors than an average child. Many kid-friendly establishments can assist with the challenges faced by ASD children when it comes to the community environment.

Each county or state has resources for special needs children. Additional services can be located by using a search engine, such as GOOGLE. Typing in "Resources Guide for Special Needs Children In _____ (state and county)" will render links to many sites. Parents who take the time to research additional services and resources help their children have a smoother and less challenging transition to receive those services.

In Montgomery County, Pennsylvania, there are many places that host child–friendly festivities for ASD and other special needs children. These establishments have learned how to engage, interact, and include the special needs child. Their establishments assist with the lack of sensory skills of the autistic child and have adjusted their services and standards to accommodate these atypical children.

Some of these places include:
- Bouncetown
- Elmwood Park Zoo
- Urban Air/SkyZone/GetAir
- Public Libraries
- Bowling Alleys
- Lego Land
- Outdoor Play Areas
- Please Touch Museum
- Great Adventure
- Sesame Place

In addition to those listed, many establishments are becoming more aware of the need to accommodate ASD individuals. Many of these establishments also offer a sensory environment that has less lighting, noises and sounds, as well as offer different Sensory Areas to support or assist with the ASD individuals who displays; repetitive movements as well as an increase in anxious and impulsive behaviors.

## Making the Home Environment Therapeutic

Implementing continuous therapies in the home environment is very important for the autistic child's life. Because the child receives a variety of services in their educational placement, it is good to transfer those skills to the child's home environment to strengthen deficiencies.

Everyone in the home should be a part of the child's routine by offering a therapeutic environment to assist with the child's needs. Parents and siblings of the individual should know techniques and strategies to use with the individual in the home or community environments. The family should connect and become affiliated with a variety of strategies and interventions to assist the ASD individual with coping and complying.

ASD individuals may have difficulty processing information due to their cognitive thought processes. Individuals diagnosed with ASD may receive Occupational Therapy, Physical Therapy, or Speech and Language Therapy. All of these therapies are important, and the family can implement some creative ideas at home to assist with the ASD individual's sensory difficulties.

Here are some ideas for home-based therapies:

**Speech and Language Therapy**
- Visuals and other posts
- Picture books
- Demonstrating and social modeling
- Repeating of sounds and words (receptive and expressive languages)
- Placing objects near mouth, initiating eye contact with the ASD individual

The above mentioned things will guide and prepare the individual for; fluency, resonance or voice, seeding or articulation (forming words). The more exposure and practice that an individual who is diagnosed with ASD has, the better preparation he/she will have. Visuals, pictures, play therapy, language, as well as demonstrating the "rolling of the tongue" will support and prepare these individuals for better eye contact, awareness, as well as attempts to make sounds or form words.

**Occupational Therapy**
- Focusing on bathing
- Toileting appropriately or introducing potty training
- Life skills (baking, cleaning, cooking)
- Pencil gripping, coloring, and writing
- Bins with sensory items (beans, rice, slime, and other textured items)
- Sticker fun
- Activities with Velcro (pulling and sticking)
- Stretching, climbing, and walking

The above mentioned items will guide and prepare the individual for; learning how to balance, grip, or continue on with important life skills that are needed to function on an everyday life. These things are important so that the ASD individuals will know how to strengthen these skills so that they can utilize these muscles more than usual. Outdoor and other recreational activities are great ways of strengthening these individuals' core or midsection that involves all muscles in the areas that includes; front, back and side. Strengthening those core areas will support the individual with, being able to balance self without too many prompts.

**Physical Therapy**
- Stretching the body and having a routine
- Using a variety of methods and other strategies that consists of body movement
- Exercising
- Trampoline
- Body stimulation
- Walking and climbing (walking and climbing stairs)
- Skipping and jumping
- Yoga ball
- Sensory swing
- Family outings and additional things that consists of movement

The above activities are great ways of assisting the ASD individual with intervals of 15-30 minutes, depending on their tolerance level. The times can be incorporated into a daily routine. The routine must be consistent. If any changes need to be made, the family should prepare the individual for a change in the schedule to decrease frustration. A timer may be helpful to assist with preparation and transition times. The goal of physical therapy is to increase mobility, using numerous methods of movement, exercising and consistent body movement, as well as stimulation.

# Chapter 9
## **Common Goals to Work On**
*"Most Effective and Appropriate Goals to Focus"*

Working with and learning the ASD child can be challenging. It is detrimental for parents and professionals to compare these children to others or to assume these children are on a certain level when they are not. No matter the length of time parenting or the number of certifications a professional possesses, servicing children with Autism Spectrum Disorder is a learning experience. Every ASD child is different, and they all have a different set of needs.

Depending on the severity of the misbehaviors, as well as the development of the child, the most effective strategies are selected to assist children with the ASD diagnosis. Children who are diagnosed with ASD display various combinations of behaviors, such as off-task, defiant, noncompliant, unfocused, hyperactive, impulsive, and cross boundaries behaviors. Learning the appropriate languages, approaches, goals, and strategies to implement helps parents, siblings, school staff, and other people who are a part of the treatment and everyday lives of the ASD child.

*Social Skills*

Improving social skills may be the most common goal for professionals treating children diagnosed with Autism Spectrum Disorder. These children often have delayed verbal and social skills. The severity of their social skill development ranges from non-verbal to being able to communicate and verbalize without the capacity to express their thoughts and feelings. Successful communication is dependent on social skills. As a result, this goal is commonly an essential part of the treatment plans of children diagnosed with Autism Spectrum Disorder.

Lacking social skills can be very frustrating and overwhelming to ASD individuals and the individuals who work with them. The ASD individual becomes extremely frustrated when no one can understand them. The individuals working to understand the ASD individual are challenged with an inability to decipher their requests. Autistic individuals are unable to regulate their thoughts and feelings, rendering them unable to express them. Instead, they become withdrawn, frustrated, and aggressive towards people who are unable to understand what they are requesting.

## *Remaining on Task/Focused*

Keeping the ASD child encouraged and focused is another common goal. These children may have a combination of ADD (Attention Deficit Disorder) 314.00 in DSM IV (2010) or a combination of ADHD (Attention Deficit Hyperactive Disorder) 314.01 in DSM IV (2010). Individuals with each of these diagnoses exhibit a lack of attention or little to no attention span. These children often zone out because they are not focused or cannot keep still. Most times, a child who has a variety of diagnoses has difficulty completing academics and other tasks. It is important to implement effective strategies to keep the child engaged, focused, and on task.

*Physical Aggression*

Some children diagnosed with ASD may exhibit ongoing physically-aggressive behaviors. Sometimes the behavior is intentional, while at other times, the actions are involuntary. The intentional types of physically-aggressive behavior occur when the child reacts on impulse or becomes fixated on objects that they feel can be aggressively taken. The unintentional aggressive behaviors can be a result of the frustration of not being able to express their wants or needs. These physically-aggressive behaviors can be a result of escape or avoidance and may escalate because of their inability to get others to understand why they decided to become physically aggressive. When a child becomes physically aggressive towards others, the parent or professional should create proximity boundaries to keep the child from harming others.

*Verbal Aggression*

Some children may show signs of verbally-aggressive tendencies. Yelling, screaming, whining, or making inappropriate and derogatory statements are verbally-aggressive behaviors. There are times when children say things intentionally to get a reaction. Some ASD children are merely reacting to the impulses when they exhibit aggressive behavior. They may feel they are losing control and become verbally aggressive as a result of that feeling of helplessness. A verbally-aggressive child could say any of the following: dummy, idiot, stupid, or I hate you. When the child becomes severely verbally aggressive, he or she will start using inappropriate language and profanity.

## *Proximity and Personal Boundaries*

Personal boundaries are one of the main goals in the treatment plans of ASD children. Many ASD children invade the space of others. Therefore, helping them understand the importance of proximity and personal boundaries is imperative to their social success.

Autism Spectrum Disorder children require those responsible for their treatment to set personal boundary limits and expectations. Sometimes they intentionally violate the space of others, but it is usually unintentional and may result in physically-aggressive behaviors. It is necessary to redirect the child and model appropriate behavior continuously. An effective strategy is placing your arm in front of you and explaining to the child that they should not cross that area. The child may continue to cross boundaries and invade others' personal spaces, requiring the parent to model the correct behavior for him or her repeatedly.

# Chapter 10
# **Different Levels**
## *"Depending on Behaviors and Sensory"*

Having been exposed to Autism Spectrum Disorder and its diagnosis for nearly eleven years, I have gained an understanding of the category and levels in which children would be categorized based on their behaviors and sensory concerns. I am also familiar with setting goals and determining what strategies are effective and appropriate.

The categories and explanations that follow are my findings. This is how I categorize ASD children to assist with appropriate treatment plan goals and effective interventions and strategies. My recommendations are based on what I observe and how the child exhibits specific behaviors and sensory concerns.

Comparing children is challenging. Even if they experience the same or similar behaviors, there still may be some behaviors that fall into a different category. The levels of tantrums or meltdowns that children experience can be compared, but other sensory concerns, behaviors, or barriers must also be considered. These additional concerns may place the child in different categories. Slight Mild, Mild, Slight Moderate, Moderate, and Severe are the levels that I often use to help me with the implementation of strategies.

**Slight Mild**

Slight Mild level is for the high-functioning Autism Spectrum Disorder individuals who are very sociable and able to verbalize as a typical individual. These individuals typically use five or more words in a sentence and can hold a fairly decent conversation about real-life events. Their good neurological thought process determines the decision to place individuals in this category in a regular education classroom setting. Engaging and interacting occur with these individuals, even if it is not as often as it could be. Some people with ASD prefer to be alone but can distinguish appropriate times to engage with others without prompting. Even though these individuals may exhibit behaviors of the average individual, they still have slight signs of decreased self-expression and sometimes struggle to express their thoughts and feelings. Tantrums and meltdowns do occur in the Slight Mild category, but the intensity, duration, and frequency do not exceed fifteen minutes. The onset of the outburst might be because of the day they are having or triggers that have occurred. These individuals understand expectations and responsibilities, even though they may have their moment of displaying noncompliant behaviors. When an ATEC Assessment is completed on this individual, scores are usually within the range of 45 to 62.

**Mild**

High-functioning ASD individuals with limited social skills may fall into the Mild category. These individuals can verbalize phrases and sentences like a typical individual but may lose confidence in their response. These individuals can use at least five or more words to form a sentence. They are capable of holding a conversation about real-life events but might be off-topic with quirky topics or things that occurred from years ago. The individuals who are in this category have the potential to be placed in a regular education classroom setting but may receive additional special education services or other therapies to assist with their sensory concerns. While they may prefer to stay to themselves, these individuals engage and interact at appropriate times.

Even though these individuals may exhibit behaviors of the average individual, they still struggle with self-expression and being able to express their thoughts and feelings. These individuals may require constant reminders using strategies such as prompting, redirecting, and implementing visual cues to help them communicate their thoughts. Tantrums and meltdowns do occur. The intensity, duration, and frequency may last up to thirty minutes. The duration of the tantrum or meltdown may increase if the individual is seeking attention or struggling to comply with instructions and strategies. Frustrations may occasionally lead to these ASD individuals losing self-control and becoming destructive and verbally or physically aggressive. Autism Spectrum Disorder individuals in this category understand expectations. They continue to display noncompliant behaviors because they feel they are right about everything. When an ATEC Assessment is completed on this individual, the score will be within the 63 to 72 range.

**Slight Moderate**

Slight Moderate is the third level and designated for ASD individuals who are not very aggressive physically but may exhibit verbally aggressive behaviors occasionally. Yelling, screaming, making threats, and using language with inappropriate content are associated with this level. These individuals are challenged and struggle with their social skills. They are not able to verbalize phrases and sentences like a typical individual. As a result of their inability to express themselves, they communicate poorly with others. The individuals who are in this category are itinerant students. They can be placed in regular education classroom setting periodically throughout the day. This flexibility allows them to transition to the ASD Classroom environment for sensory needs as needed. This leniency provides a comfortable environment for them to calm down and express themselves with the use of appropriate strategies and manipulatives.

Lack of peer or sibling interaction is common for these ASD individuals. They prefer to be left alone when given a choice. However, there are times when they want to engage in a conversation or playtime with those around them. Consistent reminders, including prompting, redirecting, and visual cues, will be necessary to assist them when communicating with others or trying to express themselves. In this category, tantrums and meltdowns last approximately twenty-five to forty-five minutes. Factors affecting the varying levels of intensity and frequency include what type of day they are having, the reason for the tantrum, and the antecedents that may have occurred. It is not uncommon for these ASD individuals to struggle with self-control and become destructive or aggressive in each of their environments three to five times a week. These individuals have a minimal understanding of expectations. When an ATEC Assessment is completed, the expected score for this level is 73 to 84.

## Moderate

The fourth level, Moderate, indicates the ASD individual is nonverbal and unable to express their thoughts and feelings. These individuals are only able to use one-word expressions. The extent of their vocabulary is five to ten words. These individuals often display aggressive behaviors. Verbal aggression is demonstrated by yelling, screaming, making different noises or sounds to communicate, and physical aggression results in biting, pinching, kicking, or hitting. They are overwhelmed by their inability to communicate with others or to express their thoughts and feelings. These individuals are not able to verbalize at all. A PECS (Picture Exchange System) helps these nonverbal individuals with communicating their wants and needs visually. The individuals who are in this category are in the ASD classroom environment full-time. This ensures their sensory needs are met and provides a comfortable environment for them to remain calm and express themselves. The appropriate strategies and manipulatives are often implemented from their I.E.P.

There is no peer or sibling interaction. These individuals prefer to be left alone and refuse to interact with others. Prompting, redirecting, and visual cues will assist them with what they want to say or express. Tantrums and meltdowns do occur, but the intensity, duration, and frequency increases by ten to fifteen minutes from the previous level. It is challenging for them to request what they want or need. The tantrum and meltdowns can continue for forty or more minutes. As with the preceding levels, the length of the tantrum is dependent upon the type of day they are having, the reason for the tantrum, the triggers encountered, or the inability to express something. It is also possible that the individual is seeking attention or having challenges complying with instructions.

On this level, the ASD individual may escape any area. They may not understand or accept the strategies and interventions that have been modeled and taught to them. Visual aid postings may assist the individual in following a routine. If the routine is not followed, the entire day may be off. Failure to maintain the schedule can cause these ASD individuals to struggle with self–control. Destructive and aggressive behavior will occur from time to time. It can happen as many as five or more times a day in any environment. These individuals cannot comprehend expectations and are unable to process more than a one or two-step directive. Their ATEC Assessment score is usually between 85 and 97.

**Severe**

This is the final level and reserved for ASD individuals with multiple diagnoses. These individuals struggle with sensory concerns, noncompliance, and attention span issues, and they can be severely impulsive, hyperactive, destructive, aggressive, as well as strays on many occasions. These individuals are nonverbal and unable to express their thoughts and feelings. These individuals have a very limited vocabulary, consisting of three to five words. These individuals display severe levels of aggressive behaviors and require numerous coping and therapeutic items. These items include fidget spinners, fidget cubes, chew toys, manipulatives, and weighted vests or blankets. The goal of coping and therapeutic items is to assist the ASD individual with the self-calming and de-escalation processes.

These individuals may also be sound- or light-sensitive. It is imperative to have specific lighting and headphones for these individuals to decrease frustration, aggressive behaviors, and tantrums or meltdowns that may escalate when they struggle to express themselves. The ASD individual is often unable to cope with the reinforced strategies. These individuals are fearless, unpredictable, and find ways to escape/avoid when they refuse to complete a specific task or activity. A PECS (Picture Exchange System), whether it is a book or licensed system on an electronic tablet from the school district in which your child resides, is very useful when the nonverbal child is unable to communicate their wants and needs. The children in this category receive their educational instruction in an ASD classroom environment. This setting is equipped to meet their sensory needs. It provides a comfortable environment for them to calm down and express themselves with the use of appropriate strategies often implemented from their I.E.P. Individuals in this category may attend an approved private school if the home school district is unable to meet the needs of the child. This option is available to offer support after all the strategies are adjusted, the I.E.P. revised, and if the individual is still not making progress.

These individuals have no peer or sibling interactions. As with the previous category, their preference is to be left alone. They refuse to interact with others. Various strategies to assist them with expressing their thoughts and needs are prompting, redirecting, planned ignoring, and squeezing their hands together. The implementation of visual cues will also help them with communication. Severe tantrums and meltdowns occur and may last over forty-five minutes. As indicated in all the categories, the intensity, duration, and frequency are dependent on the type of day they are having, the reason for the tantrum or meltdown, the antecedents experienced, or the inability to express what they want. Tantrums may occur two to four times daily across settings. It does not matter whether they are at school, home, or in the community. The tantrums frequently occur because they require consistent interventions to ensure safety and reinforce self-calming skills. These ASD individuals may escape areas despite appropriate and effective strategies and interventions that have been modeled and taught to them. Visual aid postings may assist the individual in following a routine. Consistency is vital. If the routine is not followed, their entire day will be off. Change causes frustration and can lead to these ASD individuals losing their self-control and becoming destructive or aggressive. This can happen over five times a day. These individuals do not understand expectations and can only process one to two-step directives. Their ATEC Assessment score is usually 98 to 100.

## Similarities and Differences of All ASD Levels

Most ASD individuals, no matter what level they are categorized, struggle with sensory concerns, noncompliance, refusals, elopement, frustration, hyperactivity, impulsiveness, low attention span, sound or light sensitivity, avoidance, and spontaneity. Regardless of their level, individuals diagnosed with ASD display some combination of the behaviors detailed. Even those who are high functioning, also known as ASPERGERS ASD individuals, may exhibit signs of struggling with mild sensory, noncompliance, hyperactive, or avoidance issues when presented with activities in which they do not want to engage.

# Chapter 11
## <u>Crisis Identification</u>
### *"What Antecedents Took Place"*

When a child loses all control and becomes physically aggressive, it doesn't mean the ASD individual is going through a crisis. When an ASD individual feels abandoned or unsupported, they may become emotional, use obscene language, make verbal threats, become aggressive, or leave the area. This is not a crisis. A big meltdown can be avoided if appropriate strategies are implemented to de-escalate the individual.

A crisis is a specific time when an individual is experiencing difficulty, trouble, or danger. During these times, it is challenging for them to understand safety and control when strategies are implemented.

At times, local law enforcement has been dispatched due to safety concerns, aggression, destruction, emotions, and instability. Law enforcement usually recommends calling the local CRISIS number. Personnel on the CRISIS hotline will ask a series of questions to assess the situation. They may recommend taking the individual to a hospital or a partial hospital for an intake or evaluation. Depending on the findings, the ASD individual may be admitted, have outpatient therapy, or be recommended for additional BHRS wraparound services.

## Things to Look for

Parents and caregivers must continually observe children who have Autism Spectrum Disorder. Just like other children, they have their ups and downs. Some days are more challenging than others and may require assistance to de-escalate and maintain a safe and calm environment. Notate if a child displays any unusual behavior, including unsafe behavior, changes in mood, or disinterest in preferred activities, and consider therapy if there is an increase in these behaviors. If these changes interfere with the child's favorite recreational activity, academics, or their regular daily activities, they may be in the beginning stages of a crisis.

Caretakers and/or staff should attempt to use the following techniques when a client is becoming frustrated and overwhelmed: proximity control, planned ignoring, behavior blocking, and quiet room/quiet time, as appropriate. These strategies are often useful when the individual becomes severely agitated, engages in self-harming behavior, vocalizes aggressively, or engages in aggressive behavior. Dim bright lights and silence noises to minimize sensory input. Removing task demands and implementing visuals will assist with calming the individual down, establishing a safe and trusting environment.

## List of Crisis Contacts

- **Friends Hospital at (215) 831-2600**
  4641 Roosevelt Blvd. Philly. PA 19124
- **Montgomery County Emergency Service, Inc.: (610) 279 – 8100 or 1(800)-452-4189**
  50 W. Beech Drive, Norristown, PA 19403
- **Brook Glen Behavioral Hospital: 215-641-5300**

7170 Lafayette Ave., Fort Washington, PA 19034

- **Horsham Clinic: 215-643-7800**

722 East Butler Pike, Ambler, PA 19002

- **Access Child and Adolescent Mobile Crisis Services:** 1 (888) 435 – 7414

500 Office Center Drive, Suite 100 Fort Washington, PA 19034-3234

## SUICIDE PREVENTION HOTLINE: 1(800) 452 – 4189

It is recommended that the above telephone numbers should be posted in different areas so that if an emergency occurs, an individual will have access to make necessary calls, if needed. If the above numbers aren't in your area or location, please start researching through a search engine such as; GOOGLE. If not, your Medical Insurance Provider can assist you with a list of participating and local places that best fits the individual who may need it.

## The Four Levels to a Crisis Plan

There are four levels to a crisis plan that will determine which category the ASD individual is exhibiting. The four levels are from the least concerning to the most concerning because of the severity of the destructive and aggressive behaviors.

## Level 1:

### Example of Client's Behaviors

When an individual becomes defiant or noncompliant, the behaviors the individual usually displays are off-task, whiny, emotional, anxious, slightly aggressive, hyperactive, and impulsive. As a result of an inability to self – regulate and express their wants and needs, tantrums are displayed. This individual becomes very angry and emotional. During this first level, tantrums last anywhere from fifteen to twenty minutes; depending on his/her mood and antecedents that occurred. The parent or caregiver should encourage the child to relax and calm down. The Squeezing Hands Together Strategy is effective in this level, being that it gives time for the individual to process and be able to give some details about the reasons why he/she is feeling this way. This will limit anxious behaviors.

### Antecedents and Known Triggers

The known triggers that occur in this level of crisis are not being able to understand expectations. When they are not able to remain focused or on task, they may get confused. Their confusing thoughts may transpire from overthinking or misunderstanding things. These individuals may feel limited and display attention-seeking behaviors until they get what they want. Planned ignoring can be implemented to decrease the individual's attention – seeking behaviors, but after about 15 minutes, try redirecting the conversation so that you are able to get some thoughts or feelings from the individual.

**Plan of Action**

1) Implement strategies and interventions, such as; redirecting, Squeeze Hands Approach, as well as offering verbal cues to eliminate the tantrums or meltdowns when they occur.

2) Encourage the individual who is experiencing them to use safe words or gestures when he requires a break or notices his high levels of anxiety transpiring. Also encourage this individual to take deep breaths to decrease the levels of anxiety.

3) Talk to the individual about the misbehaviors that were displayed to teach self-control and help them understand the consequences and explain a plan of action so that he/she will understand what's next by using; FIRST and THEN. For example; First, we will squeeze our hands and clean up the mess you made, and then we will talk about better choices for the future.

4) When finished, repeat steps, enabling the individual to understand what is happening to eliminate any forms of agitation, irritability, or off-task behaviors. This will assist individual with making better choices and using problem solving thinking strategies since they were able to get calm and focused during this first stage.

**Level II:**

**Example of Client's Behaviors**

The Autism Spectrum Disorder individual may have moments of impulsive and hyperactive behaviors that prevent them from staying focused and on task, as well as safe. These individuals are challenged with understanding and expressing their thoughts and feelings along with their wants and needs, being that they are challenged with keeping calm and safe. Level II behaviors are similar to Level I behaviors. In addition to those behaviors, the individual might throw himself on the floor or become very anxious. Types of physically aggressive behaviors displayed on this level include pulling and grabbing, as well as becoming destructive. These individuals are easily distracted by high levels of anxiety. The Ignoring Strategy is sometimes effective for Level II individuals. If ignoring is unsuccessful, a different strategy should be chosen. Any additional strategies that should be implemented are; verbal cues to assist with expressing thoughts and feelings as well as Problem Solving Thinking Strategies to assist with properly being able to think, prior to any forms of noncompliant or aggressive behaviors occur.

**Antecedents and Known Triggers**

Noticing others engaged with one of their preferred items may be a trigger that causes agitation and irritability. The individual could also be triggered by being encouraged to complete a non-preferred task, when he/she is not ready or isn't in the mood to do so. This might lead to a fifteen- to twenty-five-minute tantrum; depending on the triggers and reasons). The individual may become physically aggressive towards others when they prefer to be left alone.

**Plan of Action**

1) Redirect the individual from the preferred task and get them back on-track and task.

2) Encourage the individual to use deep breathing exercises to eliminate aggression and emotional behaviors. Along with that, implement the Problem Solving Thinking Strategy to assist with decreasing anxious and impulsive behaviors that could lead to physical and verbal aggressive behaviors.

3) Explain misbehaviors that have been exhibited with de-escalating visuals. Sometimes these individuals will require a visual to assist with deescalating.

4) When the tantrum is over, repeat the steps to decrease the individual's level of aggression and anxiety.

5) Use a coping item, bean bag or cushioned quiet area, a chew toy, weighted vest or blanket, or another manipulative to calm the individual.

6) Encourage the individual to sing a favorite song to redirect their attention and assist with soothing and comfort.

## Level III:

**Example of Client's Behaviors**

During a moderate to severe crisis level, the individual will become emotional, noncompliant, and defiant when given instructions that include a non-preferred task. Because the individual struggles with the strategies administered, lengthy tantrums and meltdowns will consistently occur on this level. During this stage of the crisis, the individual will elope multiple times and become physically aggressive. The individual may also display self-injurious behaviors. When unsafe behaviors, such as biting, grabbing, pulling, climbing, jumping, kicking, or pushing, are shown, immediate intervention is required. Implementing strategies, such as redirections and prompts, can help de-escalate an extremely emotional and hostile ASD individual. At this time, the individual may need a calm area (cushion) or to have a seat due to the moderate to severe levels of aggressive and hostile behaviors that are displayed.

**Antecedents and Known Triggers**

These individuals may struggle with noise and possibly are sound sensitive. Along with that, they may be overstimulated by the number of individuals who are present or in the proximity or area in which they are. They are unable to tolerate excessive amounts of noise or individuals that they shut down, but exhibit severe levels of noncompliance. They will be easily frustrated and challenged in noisy environments. A specific preferred item should be designated to assist with helping the individual cope during these times. This will comfort the individual, enabling them to express the reasons why they feel frustrated and helping them to calm down. A weighted blanket, vest, cushion or other coping item may help this individual decrease the noncompliance and aggressive behaviors.

**Plan of Action**

1) Contact a BHRS team member or BSC if the individual receives wraparound.
2) Encourage the individual to calm down and use problem-solving strategies that will help them with expression and de-escalation.

3) Use skills that the BHRS team implemented to redirect and encourage the individual to make good choices.

4) Encourage and talk with the individual, redirecting the conversation so they can become focused and limit physically aggressive and unsafe behaviors that are present.

5) Give the individual a coping item, weighted blanket, weighted vest, or compressions to soothe their frustrations.

6) Repeat steps and continue talking with the individual about what can be a goal that he/she would like to focus on or what Reward would he/she like to receive if they are able to earn 5 positive reinforcement points with the entire requirements, for example; de-escalation, cleaning up, getting himself/herself together, being focused and on task, being able to talk and engage, and then transitioning back to the area where he/she is responsible to be.

## Level IV:

**Example of Client's Behaviors**

Level IV is the final level of a crisis. If reached, contact the crisis hotline. There are many factors, even within Level III, that warrant and encourages the parent or professional when contacting the crisis hotline. If an individual is very emotional, unable to keep still, aggressive, impulsive, hostile, hyperactive, and noncompliant, the hotline should be contacted. On this level, the individual may also be self-injurious, suicidal, obscene, aggressive, and dangerous to themselves and others. During this time, immediate interventions and strategies are required. Typical behaviors on this level are anger, overwhelmed, off-task, defiant, noncompliant, resistant, and anxious. These behaviors will lead to the individual having multiple meltdowns lasting over an hour. Destructive behaviors are possible until the individual is calmed down. There is a lot of support that is needed, which multiple staff or family members need to be present to assist with this level. Removing unsafe items from area and trying to talk with the individual is helpful.

**Antecedents and Known Triggers**

There are no identifiable triggers that occur during this stage of a crisis. There does not have to be a trigger. Their feelings or mood may be the reason for their behavior. At this level, this individual is unable to self – regulate or express his/her thoughts and feelings. This individual is so angry, irritable, frustrated and hostile, that they are refusing to comply, focus, or even care about being safe. Their only concern is usually becoming physically aggressive with an individual to get his/her point across.

**Plan of Action**

1) Call 911 or transport the individual to the nearest emergency room.

2) Call the county's mobile crisis intervention hotline:

Montgomery County Access Mobile Crisis Hotline: 1(888) HELP-414

# Chapter 12
# Behavior Plans/Charts
## *PECS*

There are many devices or other items that can be used to help the Autism Spectrum Disorder child with communicating or requesting their wants and needs. This may be a more challenging stage than assisting the child. All ASD individuals are on different verbal and social levels. How the ASD individual responds will help determine which devices are needed to assist them with communicating.

**PECS (Book/Binder)**

PECS is a Picture Exchange Communication System that was created by mental and behavioral health professionals. Parents can also create their own PECS. The required supplies are a lot of pictures, Velcro, and time to put it together. It is important to categorize each item so the ASD individual can easily utilize it daily. The types of categories that can be placed in the PECS book are Actions, Responses, Foods, Activities, and Colors. Anything that may be important to assist the ASD individual with social and communication skills can be used.

Visual aids help the ASD individual understand the requests others are making. Usually, when using this PEC System, the ASD individual should only be given two options. This will keep the individual from being overstimulated. Too many options will frustrate them.

## The Talker (Electronic Version)

The electronic version of PECS has many features. The same categories exist in both versions, but the electronic version allows the ASD individual to listen to what they have created as far as combining words and phrases to request wants or to respond. It is usually a tablet or iPad form, which is usually effective for the ASD individual to hear what is requested. Hopefully, they will mimic the words they hear. By hearing sounds and noises, the ASD individual will learn how to use the system. There is no set timeframe. As long as the ASD individual is exposed to it across the school, home, and community settings, they will benefit from the system.

## Importance of Visuals

Understanding that some ASD individuals are nonverbal and unable to comply with directives or instructions, there are ways to assist him/her with their everyday; routine, schedule, lives, and being able to request their wants or needs. Create a schedule from the time the individual wakes up until the time they go to bed. Use no more than 3 words with a picture to identify; steps they are required to take or his/her routine on a daily basis. At times, an individual will become confused and unfocused if there is a change, but preparing him/her for the changes will decrease anxiety and off task behaviors.

The ways that a schedule can be created is as follows:

- Breakfast

- Brush Teeth

- Get Dressed

- Bookbag

- Jacket/Coat

- Bus

- School

- Free Play

- Unpack Schoolbag

- Classwork

- Lunch

- Recess

This is an example of what a daily schedule would consist of. For longer use and the ability to relocate the Schedule or other visuals for the ASD individuals, it is recommended that you laminate each piece and use Velcro in case there are any changes in routine or schedule. The goal and only way for a successful response from an ASD individual is to prepare with a schedule, with a Timer, as well as reminding or making this individual aware of any changes that may occur. Visuals can be placed throughout the academic or educational setting and the home environment, so that this ASD individual can be aware of; expectations, boundaries, as well as understand changes if there are any that may occur.

# Chapter 13
## Scenarios/Case Studies 1
*"Nonverbal/Physical Aggressive Elementary Student"*

Brennan is a ten-year-old, Hispanic, nonverbal child diagnosed with ASD, ADHD, Developmental Delay, as well as PTSD. Brennan was sexually abused by his stepfather. The abuser was removed from the home when the child was five years old. Brennan suffered brain injuries and was hospitalized for three weeks. Brennan continues to struggle with self-expression, even with the use of gestures. The only way in which Brennan can communicate is with a few gestures. He pulls people to where he wants to go and uses simple words like "hi" or "bye' when he greets. He says "run" when he is ready for a run break.

Brennan has an 8-year-old sister, who is a regular kid without a diagnosis. Brennan has no interactions with his sibling, although he is encouraged to comply and engage with others.

Brennan is a 4th-grade student enrolled in the ASD classroom, which is very appropriate based on Brennan's behavior and academics. Brennan receives a variety of additional services at school based on his I.E.P. The other services are occupational, speech and language, and physical therapy. All of the services are provided for thirty minutes once every six days. Brennan also receives wraparound services with a BSC Worker. BSC shares skills and appropriate strategies and interventions with the team, school staff, and the family so everyone can be on the same page.

Brennan functions as a 4-year-old and has an IQ of 76. He will be tested again next year during his three-year evaluation. Brennan elopes, wanders, becomes physically aggressive, and has tantrums and meltdowns lasting from twenty to more than forty-five minutes. De-escalation is a lengthy process. It takes Brennan a long time to become safe. Various strategies are used, such as redirecting, prompting, deep breathing exercises, and self-calming skills, to calm him. Once Brennan is displaying safe and on-task behaviors, he can take a break for ten minutes and is then encouraged to complete the non-preferred task that he previously avoided.

Staff is working with Brennan to engage with his peers, which he refuses to do. Brennan prefers to be left alone and enjoys playing by himself. When other children are encouraged to interact with Brennan, he runs from them. Brennan tends to become physically aggressive when coerced to do something that he does not want to do.

**Feedback/Recommendations:** Using a preferred or coping item to assist Brennan with transitions and engaging with others would be a good way to help him with these challenges.

Implementing visuals or PECS would be beneficial to Brennan. Using a reward as an incentive might help him learn to interact with others. Brennan should only be offered two choices for a reward he has earned. He will get frustrated if there are too many choices. Brennan must be shown the chosen incentive and given three to five positives that are earned. He will learn that engaging with others and completing requests will earn the reward.

# Scenarios/Case Studies 2
*"Highly Function/Asperger's Verbal Middle School Age Kid"*

Khalid is a 12-year-old African American, verbal child diagnosed with ASD, Asperger's, and ADHD due to his moderate to severe levels of hyperactive and impulsive behavior. Khalid resides with his biological mother and is the only child on his maternal side. Even though Khalid does not live with his father, he is very involved in Khalid's life. Khalid is considered an Asperger case since he displays lack of social skills and is challenged with nonverbal behaviors, such as eye contact and facial expressions, lack of coordination, preoccupations and rigid routines, repetitive and erratic behaviors, lack of emotion, and lack of cognitive behaviors. Khalid can be very social and is capable of holding an appropriate conversation with many successful sentences. However, he struggles with organizing his thoughts.

Khalid is the only child on his mother's side, but his biological father has two other children. His siblings are a 7-year-old brother and a 3-year-old sister. Khalid is very connected and bonded with his siblings and receives support and love from his father. His father is very involved in I.E.P. meetings, regular meetings, conferences, and whatever else required of him.

Khalid is a 6$^{th}$-grade student enrolled in the Itinerant Special Educational Setting and is academically approaching grade level. He is almost at a 5$^{th}$-grade reading and mathematical level. Khalid transitions to the regular educational classroom for 65% of his school day and receives about 35% in the special education setting per his I.E.P./N.O.R.E.P. recommendations and outcomes. Khalid's class was previously not appropriate because he needed additional support in certain areas. Khalid had two other I.E.P. recommendations, and his I.E.P. goals and objectives have been changed a few times. School is noticing a change with Khalid's penmanship and gripping of the writing utensil. They feel an additional evaluation is needed. The school staff is hoping Khalid will receive occupational and physical therapy to assist with his deficiencies and challenging behaviors. Khalid receives wraparound services, which a Licensed Behavior Specialist for three hours and a Mobile Therapist for two hours per week for each service utilized. The BSC works on teaching skills and appropriate strategies to the school, as well as modeling appropriate behaviors for Khalid. When he displays noncompliant, defiant, and unsafe or physically aggressive behaviors, he may experience a meltdown that can last for thirty minutes.

Khalid was hospitalized in an in-patient psychiatric hospital when he was 8-years-old for becoming extremely aggressive and his inability to control his behavior. Khalid was admitted and remained in the hospital for two weeks to complete evaluations and determine which triggers occurred. De-escalation is time-consuming after Khalid becomes severely emotional. The emotional behaviors can be controlled after redirecting, deep breathing exercises, and problem-solving strategies are implemented to assist with the hyperactive and impulsive behaviors. Once Khalid calms down, decreases his emotional reactions, and displays safe behavior, he is able to take a break for ten to fifteen minutes by talking to a hospital staff member with whom he feels comfortable. He can open up and express his thoughts and feelings and hopefully utilize the problem-solving strategies next time.

Staff works closely with Khalid to ensure safe behaviors and assists him in controlling his hyperactive and impulsive behaviors. Khalid refuses to complete assignments at times, instead choosing to entertain and put on a show for others. At times, Khalid interacts and approaches others so he can engage in conversation and interaction with others, and other times, he enjoys playing by himself.

**Feedback/Recommendations:** Positive Reinforcement is a strategy that can be successfully used. Using the School Base Behavior Chart is appropriate since Khalid is a high-functioning ASD child who understands expectations and consequences. If Khalid is struggling and needs some minor adjustments with the current School Behavior Chart, the BSC and school can work closely to make changes that will be effective and efficient to his current goals and daily routine.

# Scenarios/Case Studies 3
## *"High Functioning High School Student ~ Challenging with Proximity and Boundaries"*

Mack is an 18-year-old Caucasian, verbal young adult diagnosed with ASD and ODD due to his moderate to severe levels of hyperactive, impulsive, and defiant behavior he displays throughout the day.

Mack resides with his biological parents and siblings, who are very involved in Mack's daily life and treatment. Mack is encouraged to participate in recreational activities and programs, in which his family invests. Mack usually enjoys playing football and basketball, which allows him to burn the energy that builds up within him. His care team encourages him to dispose of that energy. Mack's 15-year-old sister, Katie, is in high school, and his 21-year-old brother, Russell, will complete college next year. Both siblings play important roles in Mack's life and are encouraged to spend time with him regularly, which will help him display appropriate behavior.

Mack is a high-functioning young adult enrolled in a private school to assist with his severe levels of aggressive behaviors, inappropriate language, wandering, and crossing boundaries. Mack's home district was not able to assist with Mack's needs in the school environment. Mack has met all his developmental milestones on time. Mack was sitting up by six months old, crawling by seven months old, walking by one year old, talking by the time he was two years old, and potty-trained by three years old.

Mack struggles with appropriate social skills and inappropriately uses profanity. Mack doesn't display these social skills intentionally but repeats things previously heard. Mack can express his thoughts and feelings using successful sentences. He is very social and can hold an appropriate conversation with many successful sentences. Mack is challenged with organizing his thoughts as they are spoken, especially when he is off-topic.

Mack is a 12$^{th}$-grade student in a private school setting. According to the IDEA Act and due to Mack's current placement, he is eligible to receive an additional three years of education to prepare him for adult life after graduation. Mack is not academically approaching grade level; he is almost at a 3$^{rd}$-grade reading and 2$^{nd}$-grade mathematical level. Mack has I.E.P./N.O.R.E.P. recommendations and outcomes. His current placement is very appropriate for him. Mack's I.E.P. goals and objectives consist of social skills, being focused, and staying within proper boundaries and proximity. Mack becomes preoccupied and fixated on certain things and people, and then reacts with hyperactive behavior. Mack receives occupational and physical therapies to assist with his deficiencies and challenging behaviors. Mack also is enrolled in a community-based program offered by the school that provides support with teamwork, team building, social skills, participation, engagement, programming, greeting, expectations, learning the community, and work skills. Mack receives wraparound services with a Licensed Behavior Specialist for three hours and a TSS Worker in the home for eight hours a week. The BSC works on teaching skills and appropriate strategies to the school and modeling appropriate behaviors for Mack, encouraging him to stay within proximity and boundaries. The TSS Worker in the home environment focuses on boundaries, redirecting and assisting with preoccupations and fixations with people or things.

During the I.E.P. meeting, BSC asked some questions regarding Mack's future and the last three years in the private school setting. BSC asked about OVR (Office of Vocational Rehabilitation) and preparing Mack for employment when he graduates high school in three years. Along with that service, BSC inquired about IDS (Intellectual Disability Services) to help with additional support in the community that assists with behavioral health and adult preparedness.

Staff works with Mack to assist him with transitioning and making sure he engages appropriately with others. During Mack's most challenging days, he may require one-on-one support to help with a successful school day, especially when he is transitioning or engaging with peers, due to his severe levels of hyperactive and aggressive behaviors.

**Feedback/Recommendations:** Keeping a data tracker will help parents and caregivers prepare for a F.B.A. or other observation meeting. Replacement behaviors, goals, and current behaviors are important to track so that everyone is aware of the frequency, intensity, and duration of each concerning behavior or event. Positive Reinforcement is a strategy that can be successful. Redirections are imperative, especially when Mack is crossing boundaries, uses offensive language, or is off-topic.

# My Collaborating Journey

**Professional Findings and Attributes**

This has been a very challenging, positive, educational, patient, but most importantly a blessing journey. I'm grateful to have almost 20 years of experience in the Human Services Field, which 11 years dedicated as a Licensed Behavioral Specialist; specializing in Autism Spectrum Disorder.

At first, when I heard the term Autism, I didn't know what to think. There were so many different arguments and opinions that I heard such as; "It is environmental", "It is genetic", or "It is a result of immunizations". No matter what I heard, I took it upon myself to learn about ASD also known as Autism Spectrum Disorder with ways that I could engage different strategies and tools, without thinking about how it began.

Just like everyone else, I have a mission. My mission is to always use appropriate strategies when engaging with the individual cases I was dedicated to or am responsible for. Along with that, my mission is to assist many; caretakers and or professionals with the support in creating Behavior Programs or Visual Programming for these ASD individuals. These programs will serve as a tool that he/she can use at all times.

Working with over 40 Autistic individuals from 2 – years – old to 21 – years – old, I noticed that all are different and require different needs. You can assume that one individual is the same, but guess what, you are wrong! Some are similar but never the same. There are different; levels, behaviors, behavior patterns, sensory needs, levels of social skills, coping skills needed, strategies and interventions required, and more. With each item mentioned, there are different (frequency, duration, and intensity) levels of each behavior listed above. I remind caretakers and guardians that they cannot compare their ASD offspring with another offspring, family member, or friend. All individuals are different, which getting to know him/her, is the most effective treatment that they can receive and benefit from.

I have worked with all levels of ASD individuals. About 60% of the population being nonverbal or limited ability to forming words or phrases, about 15% of the population with limited social skills with being able to verbalize, but stutters and gets stuck on specific words that he/she is attempting to express or self – regulate, and about 25% of the population that are highly functioning and able to hold great conversation that is appropriate and efficient. No matter what level that the ASD individual was or is currently on, I have always made visuals to assist him/her with cognitive thinking and sensory processing a schedule, being able to request wants and needs, as well as the visuals serving as a reminder of daily expectations.

To sum up the professional background of my last 11 + years as a Licensed Behavioral Specialist, as a professional, I would like to remind other professionals that; we have to encourage, individualize plans for each ASD person, create programs, follow goals, as well as communicate and be patient because everyone is different and serves a purpose.

**Personal Attributes**

At first, writing this book for many years and making sure that everything was detailed enough for the reader to understand, I didn't want to use many clinical terms. Instead, I created a Terms and Definition Page, in the rear of the book for a better understanding of some of the terms, that a parent may come across, which is used throughout the book.

When I began writing this book, I was focused on the professional aspect of ASD (Autism Spectrum Disorder) being that I couldn't compare or understand that there was a discrepancy with; being a professional and actually raising and residing with an ASD individual.

Back in 2017, when my youngest child was diagnosed with ASD (Autism Spectrum Disorder), it put me in a different place, which to me was a more appropriate and understanding place as a mother. I understood as a professional what things needed to be worked on with individuals who I created Treatment Plans and Functional Behavioral Assessments for, but never really could relate to those parents, prior to that.

My first signs and observations. When Tyler was about 13 months, I noticed a lot of sensory things going on with Tyler such as; constant movement in preferred places, becoming preoccupied with specific objects, watching light fixtures and ceiling fans by following them with his eyes; not his head, spitting, walking on his tip toes and etc. I thought to myself, "No I will not assume and diagnose Tyler, however, I will watch his milestones and levels of development". I wanted to track these behaviors to see if they would change (progress, regress, or become a concern), but they remained the same.

Being a professional it isn't ethical or appropriate to diagnose your offspring. The reason being that is sometimes parents may become too focused and preoccupied, misdiagnose, or overlook things, which is why it is recommended that you get a professional to assist you. Tyler was about 2 and ½ years old when he was diagnosed with Autism Spectrum Disorder. Tyler received Early Intervention Services (Occupational Therapy, Physical Therapy, and Speech and Language) Services which were very helpful. When Tyler turned 3 – years – old, his services transitioned to the Montgomery County Intermediate Unit which he then received the same services, but with different goals to focus on. At the age of 4 – years – old, Tyler was enrolled in a part day Developmental Delay Classroom Environment at that time. Tyler enjoyed his school. Once Tyler was getting closer to 4 and ½ years of age, he transferred into a different program that would assist him with his needs and decrease his elopement.

With all of Tyler's behaviors, they consisted of; aggression, off task, hyperactive, anxious, wandering, unsafe (climbing and jumping), as well as eloping. Tyler was definitely a good runner. Tyler started out nonverbal, but now is attempting to use one word; here and there. Tyler uses PECS and a Talker for communication of his wants and needs. Tyler understands everything that is being said, but tries attempting to ignore and ending with a smile.

The strategies that are most effective with Tyler are redirection, using a coping item to assist him with transitioning or compliance, as well as planned ignoring because of the severe levels of attention – seeking behaviors he exhibits. As a mother of an ASD child, I had to create many schedules for Tyler; eating, playing, and sleeping. Without a schedule being in place, Tyler would be very off task and uncontrollable.

# Conclusion

Will there ever be a cure for Autism? Will parents continue to implement a variety of strategies and interventions with the individual diagnosed with this exceptionality, to assist and support them with daily requirements? Will professionals continue to network and research a variety of programs for individuals who are on the ASD spectrum? Will caretakers ensure appropriate and safe recommendations focusing on goals, while networking with other caretakers regarding individuals on the ASD spectrum?

As a mother of an ASD son diagnosed at the age of two, I, along with my family, have built a connection, supported, created, bridged gaps, as well as shown patience while learning the life of an ASD individual. It has been both time-consuming and educational. The hands-on experience has made us feel comfortable with the strategies that we use in the home. We believe Tyler will succeed as long as he understands his expectations, boundaries, and consequences, just as if he were an average kid.

Working with ASD individuals as a Licensed Behavioral Specialist for the past eleven years has been a rewarding journey. I would not change it for the world. No matter how many similar behaviors and goals each ASD individual has, they are still individuals and require a behavior plan created just for them. The appropriateness of the treatment plan will determine the individual's success.

As a professional working with individuals with ASD and being a mother of an ASD individual, I have learned to assist these individuals by creating visuals and PECS, transferring skills, implementing appropriate strategies, and offering support to help with all individuals.

If you would like to learn more about the author, both on a personal or professional level, you may do so by contacting or following her at:

Ericka Wharton, M.S.; L.B.S.

Email: autisticallyawesome@yahoo.com
Website: https://www.autisticallyawesome.net

Instagram: autisticallyawesome_

Facebook: Austistically Awesome

# Appendix
# Important Terms/Definitions

Below you will find important terms associated with individuals who are diagnosed with ASD. It is important to understand what each word means.

**Antecedents** – A trigger or something that provokes an individual to exhibit a specific behavior that may cause harm.

**ASD** – Autistic Spectrum Disorder is an exceptionality that individuals are diagnosed with when they lack social skills and have sensory challenges.

**Asperger's** – A high level of Autism Spectrum Disorder when the individual is able to function as a typical individual; an individual who is on the higher level of ASD.

**Coping** – A comfort item or strategy used to help an individual remain calm and in a relaxed state of mind.

**De escalating** – A process in which an individual is significantly escalated with multiple attempts to calm him/her down with appropriate and effective strategies. There is a process to use, which this individual will have to understand expectations, plan of action, as well as safety.

**Exceptional** – Another term used for an individual diagnosed with a mental health disability.

**Executive Functioning** – The way in which an individual displays cognitive thought processes, which is control of behaviors.

**F.B.A. (Functional Behavioral Assessment)** – An assessment that is completed over a period of time to collect data regarding an individual's behaviors. The data is collected and replacement strategies are implemented to help individuals with appropriate treatment.

**I.E.P.** – Individualized Educational Plan consists of goals, objectives, the IQ, and assessments that were used to collect data. I.E.P. is a law-abiding document that allows an individual who would require special educational services to see what services the individual is approved for based on the assessments administered.

**N.O.R.E.P. (Notice of Recommendation of Placement)** – The part of the I.E.P. meeting/review that is usually the last thing furnished. This collection of data shows whether or not an individual is regressing in the current academic placement. This N.O.R.E.P. is signed if the caretaker approves the setting and shows what the current recommendation for educational setting is required for student. It determines if they need a change or if they will stay where they currently are placed.

**Non-Preferred** – Non-preferred is a clinical term used for when there are tasks or instructions that an individual particularly does not want to do or follow.

**PECS (Picture Exchange System)** – This system is created for the nonverbal ASD individuals who are challenged with social skills. PECS allows an individual to communicate through visuals and pictures so requests can be made for their wants and needs.

**Preferred** – Preferred is used for a favorite item or task.

**Preoccupation** – Being fixated and focused on a specific thing or person for an extended period of time.

**Proximity** – Another word for boundaries to assist an individual with understanding and being aware of personal boundaries and respecting others' personal spaces.

**Sensory** – The sensation an individual receives through physical senses, such as touching, hearing, seeing, tasting, and smelling.

**Strategies/Interventions** –Strategies are used when supporting and helping an individual with transitions, following instructions, as well as ensuring safety.

# *References*

Michelson Medical Research Foundation / Groundwork / Autism Breakthrough / Autism and the Brain (Diagram) 2012

www.pattenpublications.com

www.pattan.net

https://www.autism.com/atec. Autism Treatment Evaluation Checklist (ATEC)

>Bernard Rimland, Ph.D. & Stephen M. Edelson, Ph.D.
>Autism Research Institute | 4182 Adams Avenue,
>San Diego, CA 92116 USA

Journal Developmental Neuropsychology. Vol. 33, 2008. Issue: 3. Mathematics Ability, Performance and Achievement

DSM IV (Diagnostic and Statistical Manual. (2000).

DSM V (Diagnostic and Statistical Manual. (2013)

# Dedication

This book is dedicated to my five children – Carmelo, Cara, Carly, Ty, and especially Tyler, who was diagnosed at the age of two with ASD and ADHD. All four of my other children have been extremely patient and loving towards Tyler. They have come to understand and learn about this disorder and what affect it has on Tyler. All of them have deep compassion for their younger brother. My children have learned a lot from me with transferring different skills and strategies to use with their brother. Tyler has given my children the opportunity to understand the importance of the key term "PATIENCE" when it comes to learning and figuring out an alternate approach and effective strategies in the home and community environments that are useful to Tyler's everyday life.

As time goes on, their education and awareness about ASD will improve and progress. My children will come to understand that learning something new every day is a bonus, that this is a never-ending learning experience for Tyler as he gets older.

www.ingramcontent.com/pod-product-compliance
Lightning Source LLC
Chambersburg PA
CBHW042116100526
44587CB00025B/4078